The Long of it

Insights and Reflections

Rev. Canon Dr. S. E. Long

Foreword

The Rt. Hon. the Lord Molyneaux of Killead K.B.E.

The Title of the Book is from the Old and Apt saying, *"The Long and the Short of It."*

Slieve Croob Press
Northern Ireland

First published in 2009 by Slieve Croob, available in the United Kingdom and Republic of Ireland from Slieve Croob Press, and worldwide at slievecroob.blogspot.com.

ISBN: 978-0-9561577-0-6

Printed and bound in the United Kingdom of Great Britain and Northern Ireland.

Cover Photo: 'The Windy Gap', Slievenaboley Road, County Down, by Gary McMurray www.flickr.com/photos/garymcmurray

DEDICATION

For Ellie

HOUSE OF LORDS

LONDON SW1A 0PW

I regard it as a privilege and pleasure to commend the worth and work of my good friend Ernest Long. In this splendid book, he tells the story of his life and of a prolific writer whose work has been published worldwide.

Those of us who have long enjoyed his company and profited from his wise counsel, commend the book, not least for its insights and memorable contributions to serious thought on matters of consequence to him and us.

It is tastefully produced and illustrated and will be read with much benefit to the reader. I heartily commend the author and wish him well as he continues his ministry by the written word.

The Rt. Hon. the Lord Molyneaux of Killead KBE

ACKNOWLEDGEMENTS

I have much enjoyed time spent, and memories enhanced, in the company of so many whose friendship stimulated thought often with practical effects on me and my work. Advice and encouragement were given freely and sensitively so that I am constantly indebted to them and especially thankful to Helen Beattie, Martin Moffett, Gordon McMullan, Billy Neill and Stanley Gamble in the production of this book. They know how much I valued their assistance.

PREFACE

This is not an autobiography. It is without the minutiae of such a work. It does not dwell on family origins, to spend space on detailed descriptions and analyses of a heritage which is minus prominent persons and extraordinary exploits.

I have a good reason to be proud of my parentage and family background, humble and undistinguished, but markedly hard working, honest and honourable people. They were sensible and sensitive, in their attitudes and responses to others whose reciprocation was expected and effected in a neighbourliness which was a characteristic of their times.

The intention to economise in the use of words was to ensure that what is written conveys precisely and sufficiently the thoughts of this writer.

This applied to the incidental experiences of childhood and youth, for in a autobiography they would be featured, cited, and names named as players and sharers in the big things that happened to little people in distant days and another very different age.

I have sought to minimise the recall by telling enough to allow readers to use their imaginations and the information available to them, for local and social historians have provided them with much written, pictorial and internet material to put flesh on the bones of what I say of that period.

There are experiences, events and encounters in life about which it is better to be silent than to speak, not to avoid reference to, or remembrance of someone or something, but because there are no words that would fit them satisfactorily.

Omissions from the book are deliberate for there is that ultimate privacy, the cloak of personality; the inner self hidden from sight and sound.

I have been fortunate with relationships and friendships for in them there is mutual respect, regard and trust. That has been a theme on much I have written, for sharing our lives is essential to us. Aloneness is never easy to bear.

If I have one personal distinction it must be that I was the first man from a working class background to be ordained in the Church of Ireland. It has been said that I opened the door for many such men who followed me into the ministry of the church.

Rev. Canon Dr. S. E. Long
2009

CONTENTS

1

THE FORMATIVE YEARS

Whether they are to be seen as serious, frivolous or just ridiculous, these reminiscences begin with a fortune teller and me. I was about thirteen years of age when Aunt Aggie persuaded me, as I was about to leave the house to go with my pals, to stay and have my fortune told. My refusal was over-ruled, escape prevented, I sat across a little table from the fortune teller who "read the cards." As she handled them one card appeared to bother her. After lifting and laying it a few times she told me, "that card never appeared to me before. It means that you are going into the Church." She meant priesthood or ministry. That sounded absurd to someone of my background. When I laughed at the very idea she smiled indulgently and said, "Think as you will but the cards never lie!"

When I answered the door as a lad, a gipsy asked me to buy a little lace, a few clothes pegs or cross her hand with silver. When I refused she said, "I'll tell you this anyway. You'll live to be ninety-nine." Cheeky lad I asked could she not make it a hundred. I got a tongue lashing for questioning her gift as a fortune teller. Anyway I'm still here when many of my contemporaries, colleagues, relations and friends have "shuffled off this mortal coil."

This is not an autobiography, but insights into and reflections on the way I have travelled from youth to age. It is selective in the use of its materials and reticent about naming individuals who are still around, not because they have anything to fear from someone whose literary output, prolific for a writer with a full time and fully absorbing occupation, but for the reason that his aims have always been to inform, educate and entertain rather than to pain and provoke people and the things important to them.

Born in Belfast my father was a fitter in Coombe Barbour's, Falls Foundry, for most of his working life. At heart a countryman he yearned for the open spaces of his native Magheramorne, Co. Antrim, and he took every opportunity he had to enjoy the outdoors. My earliest memories are of holidays in Magheramorne and walks in leafy suburban avenues in South Belfast on my father's hand. My mother left the country near Kells, Co. Antrim, as a teenager and so readily adapted to city life that she never again wanted to stay overnight in rural silence. They were remarkably compatible in spite of this difference of attitude and we had a happy home, were well fed, housed and clothed in the Thirties when unemployment, and very poor welfare benefits, made many hungry, cold and threadbare.

The people of the back streets of Belfast were kind to one another and sharing was common practice. Those a little better off gave or "*lent*" to the less fortunate among them. It is a regret of these affluent days that the children of parents who survived "The Hungry Thirties", and live in a style beyond parental imagination, have lost that sense of good neighbourliness. We often meet people who say "I don't know my next door neighbour" in a tone of voice which suggests that this is an advantage in living where they do.

Our school, St Philip's P.E., Excise Street, Belfast, was better known as "the Pig Crew" a nickname which embarrassed teachers and pupils and was of unexplained origin. A wee school in the days when small size schools were plentiful in Belfast, it had the distinction of having the biggest master. Hugh Campbell was a large man in height and weight. We were able to say, "We've a wee school and a big master." There were three other teachers in the two room building, Miss Gray, Miss Reid and Miss Johnston (who appeared to be the infant's teacher forever). Miss Gray and Miss Reid were opposites, the former middle aged and physically weak, and the latter young and strong who wielded the cane with vigour and pleasure. I must have gained something from them as I progressed from one to the other but it was the master who encouraged me to write. He liked my compositions and persuaded me to use words intelligently and precisely.

As I think back on my school days I am grateful for the emphasis on the "Three Rs" and particularly for a concentration on the proper use of language, our own. We were taught other subjects but the curriculum made a short list, for it was governed by few facilities and lack of accommodation. Sited in the midst of streets of houses it had no playground, just a back yard in which the toilets were located just like the houses of the pupils.

3

St Philip's schoolhouse was also a Parish hall of the Church to which we belonged St Philip's (Drew Memorial) on the Grosvenor Road, and my Sunday school. The rector was Canon Brice Coates who had a long ministry there. A Churchgoer from childhood I recall nothing that "put me off", though enthusiasm for religion waxed and waned, in what happened in the Drew Church or in Albert Street Presbyterian Church which I attended regularly after a family disagreement with St Philip's. Both churches were well attended, lively and attractive, in those days.

We boys compensated for the lack of recreational opportunities at school by playing street games after school and at all free times. There were soccer matches with the goals the space between walls and lamp posts, that's of course until a policeman appeared and the small ball was taken off by footballers who became fast runners at the sight of uniform. Other games were "Rally O", which involved a team running after individuals and catching them, and "Rounders" with a similarity to baseball. In paved streets marbles were used for several games and there was "Hop Scotch" and skipping for the girls with the difference that theirs had the accompaniment of songs and rhymes that trilled off the tongue.

2

B.B. & The Glorious Game

I found an additive to life in the Boys' Brigade which provided me with supervised fun and games and there was the discipline of the drill and the benefit of the physical exercises with clubs and dumbbells and the vaulting horse and parallel bars.

One B.B. incident with unfortunate repercussions came when the company was loaned some dummy UVF rifles for a special dress-up drill feature in an annual display. I took one home and hid it in the parlour to avoid explanations. While in its woodenness it bore only a fleeting resemblance to the real thing my mother with a native fear of firearms raised the house and street until someone explained the origin and use of the gun. For causing so much consternation and fear to her and the others I received more than adequate abuse and physical punishment.

In B.B. more than all else was the football team which played on Saturday mornings in the public parks. There were many exciting matches, a few good wins and many humiliating defeats. Strange things happened sometimes, like when one of our players in a crude tackle appeared to decapitate an opponent. The stand-in referee, a gentle, long serving member of the B.B. F.A, immediately pointed our man to "the pavilion." When we gathered around him, pleading that the tackle was awkward but not intended to hurt, and the player, who had suffered only from fright, joined us in our pleas for a reprieve, the ref relented and Bobbie Ferguson came on to finish the match. The conditions of play were primitive for the changing room was a cell with a bench and a window without glass. The pitches were quagmires in winter with the clay so deep and sticky that to move the ball more than a few yards required more strength than skill. When conditions were like that Falls Park was the place to be, for there a running stream could be used to wash off the mud. The water was icy cold but the wash was worth the shivers and usually we warmed up as we ran to get out of the park before the gates closed.

Our most frightening experience was at Victoria Park in a cup competition when our players, Victor and Ernie Dawson, were blamed for "edging the boot." They produced such anger from the opposition, and the spectators, that we were glad not to have a pavilion that day, for we had to gather up our clothes and run for our lives.

We had another experience with Victor Dawson at a practise kick about in Gribby's Field near where we lived when he tried to prevent a ball from going into the Blackstaff River. He followed head first into the smelly stream. Because his father was a strong disciplinarian and we wanted to save him punishment we lit a fire and dried his clothes. We need not have bothered for when he got home the smell of the river water gave him away and he was stropped anyway.

Living near the Blackstaff River which meandered past Windsor Park, Celtic Park, Broadway Park and Grosvenor Park it would have been nearly impossible for a young fellow not to be soccer mad. While my pals were mostly Linfield supporters I favoured Distillery and was a regular at Grosvenor Park. Though I remember exciting matches on that most compact ground we were often the losers there and at the commodious Windsor Park. It was said then that clothes horses togged out as the blues of Linfield would beat the Whites of Distillery. There was an inferiority complex at Grosvenor, accounted for by the fact that while many flocked to Windsor to watch the Blues, the Whites had only the whole hearted support of the few. Linfield was the Protestant club and Belfast Celtic the Roman Catholic one while the Distillery supporters were of both religious persuasions.

The great games of the time were between Linfield and Celtic – the Big Two – and neutrals like us were able to appreciate the many good players of both teams. The best known and most popular footballer was Joe Bambrick, from our own Roden Street, whose goal scoring feats have never been equalled. The Windsor roar was "head, heel or toe slip it to Joe." Glentoran in East Belfast had also a prolific scorer, another centre-forward Fred Roberts, who vied with Bambrick, and their supporters cried, "toe, heel or head slip it to Fred."

There were many characters in Irish football in those days. Names which come readily to mind are Jack Vernon, Harry Walker, Norman Kernoghan, Charlie Tully, Billy McMillen, Jimmy McAlinden and Bertie Fulton of Celtic and Tommy Breen who played in goal for both Celtic and

Linfield. Among the Blues were Jackie Donnelly, Eddie McCormick, Tommy Richardson and Jack Jones. Distillery had Billy McAdam, Billy Mitchell, Eddie Lonsdale and Tommy Walker. Some of them became international players and a number made proud reputations in English and Scottish football.

Billy Mitchell was one of Ireland's finest wing-halves. Early in his Distillery days he had a loss of form and was relegated to the second eleven. His team mates persuaded him that he should have it out with the manager for he was too good for reserve team football. He talked to the manager. Asked about the boss' response he said, "he told me I was in the seconds only because there were no thirds. I had no answer to that." These were the days when even the best players were paid a few pounds a week. Many, who in later and more affluent days would have made soccer their career with English and Scottish clubs; opted to follow a trade or profession and stayed at home.

My recollections of games at Grosvenor Park are many but a few experiences stand out like the games when Distillery beat Linfield by scores of five and six goals on successive weeks. It was the war years and Irish League clubs were strengthened by English and Scottish stars serving in the forces and temporarily domiciled in Northern Ireland.

I still recall one Distillery fan so hysterical with joy at the new experience shouting above the din in the second match and after the sixth goal "Score no more I've won the pools."

Guesting for the Whites were players of the quality of Rowley, Bennett, Embleton, Drury and Head.

We got many a laugh at the repartee of supporters and no club was without its wits. Sam Dempster was the Distillery man who made many memorable cracks like "That goalie of ours has such an opinion of himself one of these days he'll get his head stuck between the posts." He said of a winger, "If that fellow was charged for being a footballer he'd get off, for he's perfectly innocent." When a player was nervous in the tackle there was the call, "Give the baby a lollipop." The misnaming of opposition players and referees, who seldom went unscathed, was something else. Thick skins have always been necessary on soccer pitches.

I mentioned Broadway Park, the playing field of the junior club, Broadway United, but it was lost to housing and industrial development more than sixty years ago. Celtic Park and Grosvenor Park are also gone long since.

3

THE TOUCH OF OUTREACH

As we lived at a time and in a place much affected by evangelistic outreach from the churches and mission halls which proliferated in the city we could hardly be untouched by them and their philosophies. It happened that I had gone to Sunday School with Jack Kelly whose family had strong commitment to mission work at home and abroad, one sister was a Faith Mission Pilgrim and another was to become a missionary with the Japan Rescue Mission. His father was Sunday School superintendent in Roden Street Mission Hall and an elder in Albert Street Church. Jack was a keen young Christian and he persuaded me to attend a gospel mission service in Conway Street Hall, Shankill Road, which was under the care of Albert Street Church. The resident missionary, Samuel Walker, was the father of the Irish International Rugby football star, Sam Walker. There in the exciting atmosphere of a revivalist meeting I made a decision to put my trust in

Jesus Christ as Lord and Saviour. The decision was to affect my thinking and conduct ever after.

It brought me into the fellowship of the Roden Street Hall of the Belfast City Mission whose missionary David Forbes was a W.P. Nicholson convert. Forbes was a fine singer and choir master and fundamentalist preacher. He soon had Jack Kelly and me in the choir and on the platform as willing but very inadequate speakers. Whatever we did to our listeners we got good training in public speaking.

The strict Puritanism of the hall meant that to go to the pictures, or to smoke or to play or work on the Sabbath was condemned with make-up for the girls and every other worldly pleasure for all of us. I tried to keep the rules and was assiduous in Church and Hall attendances, prayer meetings and Bible studies. The one unfrowned on recreation was walking circumspectly after Sunday evening service when large numbers of young people paraded the Malone and Lisburn Roads courteously greeting one another and sometimes clustering for a yarn about little or nothing.

These were the days of man's innocence when having little money we enjoyed ourselves without it, and the distractions of television and games on Sunday had still to come. Those of us whose youth was spent in "The Hungry Thirties" still look back with regret that many of its values were lost before the decade ended and war came and the whole world changed.

4

WORKING OUT A CAREER

I went to work in Coombe Barbour's foundry and learned what hard graft meant for the moulding shop was the most primitive department in a firm struggling to survive. There were few mechanical aids and men and boys had back breaking chores when they made moulds and poured metal. Hard work produced hard men and some of those who worked in the foundry were hard swearers, big drinkers and obsessive gamblers. At work they were sometimes coarse and quarrelsome and after work noisy and belligerent in the pubs of the Shankill. Because I lived away from the scene I heard about the exploits of my fellow workers but saw nothing of them. I had to make the best of the job for there was little work around and few opportunities in any other direction.

Just before the War, I got a fitter's job in the Harland and Wolff Shadow Factory as a beneficiary after an arrangement of the Foundry

Worker's Union with the Amalgamated Engineering Union. The work there made few demands on physical strength and I found pleasure and profit in it for the wages were very much better than in the foundry. We worked in small squads of fitter and riveters who were mostly young fellows and classed as labourers. Most of my work in the factory was in Sterling Bombers and after a while on the bench making small parts I became a skinner of the alclad sheeting on the frames of the plane. The German blitz on Belfast in 1941 targeted the H&W factory and flattened it. It was a night attack, which meant that there was no shift on at the time and those who lost their lives were security men.

As Short and Harland had taken over the premises of the Royal Ulster Agricultural Society for aircraft production I went to work in the King's Hall. While the surroundings were far superior to anything I had seen previously and there were catering facilities unheard of at Queen's Island I had a short stay there, just until the H&W Factory was rebuilt. I left the King's Hall having been a foreman in brown coat with blue collar and lapels, to become a squad leader on a piece of work where payment was on results basis. I left that job at the end of the war when arrangements were in hand to close down the factory. The building was to be used as had its predecessor as the joiners' shop of the shipyard.

I enjoyed my work in the aircraft factory where I made many friends, but I remain puzzled by the fact that in the long years since 1945 I have met only a few of them and have no intimate knowledge of any of them. I can only conjecture that many left the country in search of work with much better prospects than appeared to be available in post-war Ulster. The strange thing is that from 1949 to 1956 I ministered in East Belfast where many of my aircraft colleagues had lived.

Because I had been a student always, an avid reader and occasional writer – my first articles appeared in the then literary orientated Ireland's Saturday Night where many writers of prose and poetry had their first experience of being published – I was able to get a good enough mark in a Trinity College Dublin examination to be admitted to the London School of Divinity, St John's Hall, temporarily at Harrow-on-the-Hill, Middlesex. I had attended evening classes in Shaftesbury House College for several years and full time 1945 and 1946 with Dr Renshaw and Mr Richard Burrows as principals.

My interest in the Christian faith had remained down the years and for many of them my often declared intention was to become a clergyman. In days when there were no church grants and the sons of artisans found entry into any of the professions very difficult my prospects were not good. The goal would have been impossible had it not been for my employment in the aircraft factory, for it allowed me to save what was needed, with some vacation employment, to pay my way through college. I had the inestimable benefit of the help and encouragement of my wife, Ellie Ferris, for we married on 16 April 1947.

'Young Love'

5

A JOURNEY IN MINISTRY

On my pilgrimage from hope to realisation I had a friend who was very important to me. He was the Rev. W.J.Gregg, minister of Argyle Place Presbyterian Church, Shankill Road, I was to describe him years later in an article as *"My Most Unforgettable Character."* He was Ellie's clergyman and officiated at our wedding. As my tutor in elementary Greek, Latin and English he gave me an understanding of languages which was necessary in my training for ordination. I was also fortunate in having Miss Betsy Sayers for Greek. I was indebted to her for the advice, that having done my best I should not criticise and denigrate myself. I found that good philosophy so that I never hold an inquest on what I have done, for worrying about what is out of one's control is a worthless exercise. It has also meant that I try to be careful in preparation of any work, and not be guilty of unpreparedness.

Billy Magee and I were students well away from the serious academic pressures of college, young men with an intention not clearly perceived by ourselves but anxious to make a start on the long road to learning, training, and trudging towards a yet unknown destination when Rev. W.J. Gregg, saint and scholar, Shankill Road, took us for studies in the subjects integral to our progress, if the ministry in the Church was to be our destiny.

The influence of that wholly committed man of God was entirely beneficial then and not just scholastically but practically and sympathetically. We never undervalued it for this was the beginning, the continuance was on to ministry in the Church for each of us, Billy to become the minister of Armagh Road Presbyterian Church, Portadown, and me a Church of Ireland Rector of Dromara and Garvaghy. We met up down through the years, for we had extra-ministerial interests in writing and broadcasting, and their effects on the progress of the faith.

Billy became a highly esteemed voice and presence on radio and television. His quiet, simplistic, personable style was an attraction for many listeners and viewers. Most regrettably he died at relatively young age to the grievous loss of so many of us.

At one of our get-togethers, years after ordination we talked of his church and mine, their similarities and differences, and he wondered about the position I was in with a bishop "looking over my shoulder" and assessing my work all the time. He was surprised to hear that the relationship of bishop and clergy in the Church of Ireland was entirely relaxed and the basis of ministry was trust and a shared obedience to the rules and regulations of the Church.

W.J.Gregg, was a fine classical scholar, expository preacher and pastor extraordinary. He was a prime example of what a Christian minister should be, self effacing and self sacrificing and without that sense of denominational exclusiveness which makes a mockery of "the whosoever will, may come" of the Lord Jesus. He was not the kind to be honoured by his Colleagues. They were lesser men whose self interest and choice of friends guaranteed them position and prestige.

W.J.Gregg whose car was available in the morning, afternoon and evening and left at the end of the road at night was the friend and confident of the tramway men whose cars carried him. In his retirement he became the Patron of the Coalmen's Mission at Donegal Quay. There were many who esteemed it a privilege to know such a man.

When I entered the London College of Divinity in 1946 it was at West Acre, a house of Harrow School. The original College at Highbury had been destroyed in a Nazi air raid and for a time St John's had been accommodated at Oak Hill College, Southgate. It was a one year stay at Harrow for in 1947 the college was located at Ford Manor, Lingfield, Surrey. The staff included Dr. Donald Coggan, Principal; Dr F.W. Drillistone, Vice-principal; and Ralph Dean, Chaplain and Senior Lecturer. "Doc" Coggan was to become successively, Bishop of Bradford, Archbishop of York and Archbishop of Canterbury; Dillistone became Dean of Liverpool and a Canon-in-residence of St Paul's Cathedral. Both men were making reputations as authors, Coggan with his work on preaching – he was regarded as a most competent exponent of the craft – *The Ministry of the Word*; and Dillistone with his *The significance of the Cross*, a study in the death and resurrection of Christ, a subject in which he was to be a widely recognised scholar. Ralph Dean became the Bishop of Cariboo, in the Anglican Church of

Canada, the second Executive Officer of the Anglican Communion, again Bishop of Cariboo and finally an assistant bishop in the Diocese of Chicago of ECUSA.

Dr Coggan was such a good lecturer that even when he had little to say he said it so well that he held our attention. Dr Dillistone was a popular and highly respected teacher, of deep spirituality who always impressed with the quiet articulation of his material. We were encouraged to think our way through the maze of theological problems to reach conclusions with which we could live. Ralph Dean had a telling turn of phrase and a style at once inspirational and practical. When Dillistone left for a professorship in Canada Dean succeeded him. Other staff members in my time included R.G.G. Hooper and Douglas Webster. Hooper, a gentle shy man is recalled as the one lecturer who read his lectures word by word and in sticking so closely to his script found difficulty in lifting his head. In spite of this we learned a great deal from someone who persuaded us of the value of serious study of Holy Scripture. Because he lectured on Higher Criticism he was often questioned as to its validity by conservative minded students. One of them had a private session with him and after a lengthy discussion in which Hooper explained the position of the Bible critics, apparently with some success, the student with his hand on the door knob turned to say, "Sir, you have made a good case for Higher Criticism and I have no answer to it but I do not believe a word of it." After his time at St John's, Hooper went back to parish work. Douglas Webster was always an enthusiastic teacher and easy to listen to. After St John's he became secretary of the Church Missionary Society and afterwards a residentary canon of Westminster Abbey. Among the part time lecturers were J.B. Phillips, the translator of the New Testament into modern language and author of several books. We had many visiting preachers, some of stature like J.W.C. Wand, Bishop of London, J.S. Whale, F.W. Kenyon, F.J. Taylor (sometime Bishop of Sheffield) and Bishop Wynne of the Sudan, M.A.C. Warren, T.W. Manson, B.F. Simpson, Bishop of Southwark. The College Visitor was J.S. Taylor, Bishop of Sodor and Man and we had visits from Geoffrey Fisher, Archbishop of Canterbury and Archbishop H.W.K. Mowll, Primate of Australia, whose bulk when he rode in the principal's Austin Seven made it so lopsided that on the passenger side it nearly trailed the ground.

My memories of West Acre are pleasant, though when there we suffered the winter of 1946-1947 one of the worst in living memory. For most of three months, nearly a term, the snow and ice prevented easy movement and drastically reduced outdoor activities. Those of us who played soccer suffered grievously for the pitches were unplayable. It is a strange quirk of memory that we forget the serious and remember the trivial. In St John's there were several long time practices some of them to do with meal times. One such was permission granted to students to speak in hall after an evening meal on any subject of choice. The right to speak did not guarantee a hearing and most of those courageous enough to make the attempt were heckled unmercifully. The heckling was usually accompanied by a blatter on tables with spoons flattened by years of such use, but when Jack Jose, the Cornishman, stood up to speak on campanology we only heard the word for everything else he said was drowned in the ringing of glasses.

Being the one Irishman in College I had better treatment when on St Patrick's Day I said something about Ireland and its patron saint. I had shamrock sent over each year and my fellow students and staff were kind enough to pin it to their gowns. And at chapel service there was a distinctive Irish flavour in prayers and hymns. I managed on two of my three St Patrick's Days to persuade the chef to cook Irish stew for dinner. The exception was when he mixed the dates and we had Indian curry on the 17th, and with apologies, the stew on the 18th. I had to run the gamut for everyone knew of my dislike of curry which was always too heavily spiced for my tender palate.

There was another experience with food when having persuaded the chef to put porridge on the breakfast menu I had it one morning tasting a bit off. When I pushed the plate to one side, and my neighbour Cliff Mason followed suit on hearing my complaint, Ralph Dean from the top of the table – the staff sat with the students at breakfast – noticed Mason's untouched plate asked, "Mason, why are you not eating your porridge?" Mason's reply, "It's off" made Dean ask "Where is that Irishman, he's the only one here who would know that?" Mason's "Beside me" was the answer the questioner anticipated.

Food rationing meant that fish was the one food more readily available. We had it in some form for dinner, tea and even breakfast at times. Like Cousin Isobel who got so much butter from the Churn as a child that she went off it for the rest of her life I have never been enthusiastic about fish dishes since 1947 to 1949.

In my Harrow days I was advantaged in being befriended by David Stephen who was in his final year. We had Belfast in common, for while he had been born in Scotland, he had lived from childhood to young manhood there, before joining the staff of the London City Mission. He and his wife, also from Belfast, and their two little daughters lived in a house at Tooting belonging to the Parish Church in which David had served as a city missionary. Mrs Stephen was my very kind hostess on weekend visits to her home. The Stephens made college life much more bearable for me. When David was ordained in 1947 it was for the curacy of St John's Blackheath, and I spent some weekends with him there. David wanted to be regarded as an Irishman, though having been born in Scotland and resident in England for several years, he had little trace of an Irish brogue. He was annoyed when his fellow students called him "Taffy" and took him for a Welshman.

St John's Blackheath showed me the Church of England at its best for the Vicar Tony Waite had a good ministry in which he had the support of many deeply committed lay people of all ages. He was afterwards Vicar of St George's, Leeds, where his pastorate was made memorable by its concentration on the social emphases of the Gospel, and the use of the crypt to serve the needs of the city's poor, hungry and homeless.

It was on a visit with David Stephen to Jim Graham, an Irishman and former LCM worker in 1947 that we heard Billy Graham. Jim was curate at Morden with T.L. Livermore, the highly esteemed English evangelical. As it was a Sunday we went to evening prayer where the American was introduced as an evangelist with great promise. Years later when I heard the famous Dr. Billy Graham he appeared to me little different in his preaching style and content from how I remembered him at Morden.

Jim Graham came to Ireland as curate-in-charge of Magherahamlet and from thence rector of Annalong. In 1967 I exchanged parishes with David Stephen for a month. He was then vicar of Alfold in the diocese of Guildford where we were to enjoy a happy holiday touring and visiting the well known resorts of Brighton, Bognor and Littlehampton and the many towns and villages around. I was able to see many fine churches and the red brick Guildford Cathedral. I wrote a series of articles, as I was known to do after visiting new places, and they appeared in The

Church of Ireland Gazette. Alfold Church was a smallish building, very old, and with several arresting features such as the granite slab of the Holy Communion Table and a pulpit which had to be mounted with care for age had made it rickety while guaranteeing its value as an antique, sounding board and all.

While West Acre and Harrow had much to commend them and Toxteth Church which was used as college chapel was a short walking distance away, we had a "built in" Chapel at Ford Manor; Dormansland, near Lingfield, when we went there for the opening term of 1947-48. The oak panelled banqueting hall of the great house made an excellent chapel when it had been appropriately furnished with fittings many of them rescued from the blitzed St John's at Highbury.

Ford Manor was the home of the Hon. Mrs Spender-Clay, a delightful elderly lady who became our very good friend. She lived in a large self contained flat in the midst of the house with her maids and butler who was especially kind to me when he discovered my origins and disclosed that he had been in the employ of the Duke of Abercorn before coming to Mrs Spender-Clay and Ford Manor where he had been for thirty years. He reminisced on his days in Ireland with obvious pleasure. The Spender-Clays were related to the Royal Family, for a daughter of our landlady was married to David Bowes-Lyon a brother of the Queen Mother.

An invitation from Mrs Spender-Clay allowed me to see the cup final of 29 April 1949 on television – not many sets were around then – when Sammy Smith, an old team mate with Albert Street Y.M. in the Churches League, scored a magnificent goal for Wolverhampton Wanderers to help them win the cup. When I asked him to get me the autographs of his team for the patients of Lingfield Epileptic Colony he sent them written on a soccer ball. We got to know many of the young people at the homes, for as students we were responsible for Sunday services and some week-day activities. One young fellow was much involved with us and he appeared to be very well with the only symptom of the disease an occasional momentary loss of concentration. We were shocked when a doctor told us that he was an exceptionally difficult case. He explained that he would become like the badly affected epileptics as he grew older. I have been reminded often that physical appearances can be deceptive.

Another invitation from Mrs Spender-Clay allowed me to view the wedding of Princess Elizabeth and Prince Philip. She was a guest at the Cathedral ceremony.

We had the use of a soccer pitch at the Colony and our home matches were played there. St John's had a proud reputation for its soccer teams performances in the Theological Colleges League. I felt highly honoured to be elected captain of the team for the 1948-9 season. The job meant more than might appear, for the captain was responsible for selecting the team and listing the names of students for practice games. Therein hangs a tale, for after supper one Saturday night – most students went home or to relations while distance people like me stayed put – I was gently ribbing Charlie Karunaratna of Ceylon who was wearing an especially colourful shirt and gaudy tie when Charlie Branch had his go but seriously. He condemned Charlie for letting down the college and belittling himself as an ordinand. Hard things were said by both men before they parted angrily. On the Monday night when I posted the list for soccer practice Charlie Branch was named. I was being naughty to punish him, for he had an abhorrence of any outdoor activity and soccer above all. He came to me annoyed at his listing and then pleading for his name to be removed. I told him I would only do that if he apologised to Karunaratna for his unwarranted attack on him after pleas of self justification the promise was made. I was in bed that night when the Sinhalese whispered in my ear, "Branch is not such a bad fellow for he has just apologised to me for what happened the other night."

The soccer captain had to apply to Mr Whittaker, the manager of Arsenal F.C. for tickets for the team's home games. When I did that I got a most kindly letter from the manager in which he referred to the long standing relationship between St John's and his club, whose ground, Highbury, had been part of the old Highbury College grounds. The association he said had been to mutual advantage. I enjoyed some exciting games, for Arsenal had a good team with the great English international Joe Mercer the star for them. We had another connection with Arsenal F.C. for Ralph Dean had played in one of the junior teams.

I attended the meeting of the Theological College Athletics Union at King's College, London, on 14 May 1948 when the London Bible College was admitted to membership. I was back again at King's for another meeting of the Union on 19 November 1948 when we amicably settled a dispute with Spurgeon's College over a postponed fixture.

R.S. Dean was a skilful winger who gave many fine performances in a team which despite several changes of personnel blended remarkably well. The principal and other staff members were generous in their support of the team. No persuasion was enough to put others of them into jersey and pants on a soccer pitch, though in one practice game Dr. Dillistone surprised us when he appeared suitably attired to have a game. He soon showed us that his superior knowledge and wide ranging studies did not include association football. He said he enjoyed the experience but never repeated it. I was very pleased when the College Sports Committee awarded soccer colours to two of us, Frank Dean, our most competent and courageous goalkeeper and myself.

The soccer league had many fine players most of them ex-servicemen with talent and flair for the game. It was said of a few of them that if they failed to be ordained they could become professional footballers.

While I remember many of my soccer experiences I recall with the greatest pleasure our matches with Oak Hill because it had Bill Seaman as a player. Bill, an Irishman, always laid on an after games meal for me in his room and I returned the compliment when his team visited us.

I watched rather than played cricket, though on occasion because St John's had a player short I was pressed into playing. A cricket match I well recall was played at a village in Buckinghamshire between a local eleven captained by the squire and St John's. The squire was a flambuoyant character who disclaimed whites choosing to play in a royal blue shirt and grey flannels with a floppy hat on his head. If he did not look like a cricketer he showed that he knew how to wield a bat. He owned the local brewery which employed nearly everybody around and was a benign tyrant compelling acceptance of his will. He was a churchwarden and expected his employees to attend church every Sunday. Just before service began he stood up in his place and surveyed the scene, absentees were called to account next day.

Travelling to and from college at beginning and end of term meant that the boat and rail trips became kind of automatic and with a few extraordinary experiences to lighten the monotony. I travelled by Heysham boat and reached London about noon a full six hours on the train. As I usually arranged to meet fellow students at Euston Station I had company for the short leg of the journies.

I had one unforgettable experience when unable to book into a two-berth cabin I had one companion a young sailor with me in a four berth one. We were out at sea before the other bunks were occupied by a couple of Tyrone men who had met after many years, a few hours earlier. They had grown up together. One of them had left the farm for a job in England and was returning from holiday; the other had gone to sea and was a mate on a cargo boat in the China seas. The seaman had a watch the friend coveted. He made offers to the more inebriated seaman who refused them. The young sailor had been attracting the attention of the seaman who asked him, "Where are you going?" "Plymouth" replied the sailor. "Do you know the big house on the hill near your depot there?" The sailor looked askance before answering, "Yes I do but the only building there is the prison." "That's it", said the seaman, "I served time there for killing a woman." Then he told the gory story of how he had come on a prostitute bleeding from a throat wound, the result of a vicious attack by a client and in pity he had "finished her off." The sailor may have slept when the cabin quietened: there was not a wink of sleep for me.

6

MY LEARNED COLLEAGUES

My indebtedness to St John's has always been apparent though I never found my lecture notes of as great usefulness as Dr. Coggan had predicted. I had learned early in life that I am not usually a beneficiary from teachers and lecturers. Their value has been to send me to the books and studies and researches for myself. Dr. Coggan was right when he said what we learned in college set us on the tramlines but the terminus was away in the distance only to be reached by our own efforts.

There were many important events and character-making experiences at college but memory being very selective and often irrational means that what was extraordinary has been lost while the ordinary persists in the mind. I recall a weekend a group of us spent with the Church Army in London 19 to 21 March 1949 and taking part in a march of witness and a meeting in Hyde Park. We went there afraid of what we might face from the hecklers. We were assured that CA would take over if things got rough, and if we went on a bit we would be pulled down. We had an eye opener seeing the CA handle the crowd and their hecklers and how they managed open air teaching and preaching with skill, tact and courage.

A highlight of my college days was the mission to St Helen's in Lancashire. The commissioning was by the Bishop of Liverpool on 1 April 1949. Accommodation was provided for us by parishioners in the case of some of us by those of the daughter Church of St Andrew. I was happily placed with an elderly couple Mr and Mrs Bert Lea at 179 Speakman Road.   St Andrew's had a lively and enthusiastic congregation many of the young people were students at Cowley Grammar School. The well prepared for mission while it had many features familiar to me there were new ideas too. One of them was more effective than I anticipated: before each meeting there was "*snap visiting*" with an earnest invitation to attend that night, and many did.

The ten days mission had a number of people declare their commitment to Christ. One of our group was to return as curate of St Helen's with St Andrew's when Bill Correy was ordained that year.

Two of us made something of an impression at St Andrew's Charles Karunaratna for his colour, and his colourful robes which he wore occasionally, and me for my brogue. Unfortunately for me when I was asked to say something in Irish I was unable to do so for I hadn't a word of the tongue.

7

ORDINATION

My ordination was on 26 June 1949 – I had been a Lay Reader with episcopal licence from 4 July 1948, during vacations, at St Aidan's, Sandy Row, Belfast – in St Clement's, Templemore Avenue, East Belfast. The Bishop of Down and Dromore, the Right Rev. William Shaw Kerr, D.D. had been most helpful to me at college, and I appreciated him as an historian who had contributed considerably to studies in Irish history of special interest to me. He was an able champion of his church in attacks from Roman Catholic and Presbyterian scholars. He was strongly Protestant and reformed in his theological thinking and readily declared himself by article and letter in local papers. His books *The Independence of the Celtic Church* and *Who persecuted?* were rated highly for scholarship and painstaking research. And he had earned a reputation for his liberal attitudes to political and ethical problems. He had a varied ministry as Rector of Ballywalter, St Paul's, Belfast, Holy Trinity, Banbridge and Dean of St

Anne's Cathedral, Belfast.　He was one of the most learned and practical of Irish bishops.

Seven ordinands were made deacon by him that day – J.R. Hall for Seagoe; T.W.W Jones and M.W. Dewar for Lurgan; D.A. Murphy for Banbridge; R.R. Cox for Dundonald; R.S. Jackson for St Finnian's, Belfast and S.E. Long for St Clement's, Belfast.　I preached my first sermon there at evening prayer.　My rector, Canon W.H.N. Fisher, had had a thirty-six years ministry in the parish when I joined him.　He was ordained in 1903 and was Curate of Carnteel, 1903 to 1905; At Luke's, Deptford, 1905 to 1906; St Thomas', Kensal Town, 1906 to 1909; Christ Church, Belfast 1909 and Rector of St Clement's 1913.　He was appointed Prebendary of Dunsford in Down Cathedral in 1946.　A bachelor, without any difficulty in understanding family problems, he showed sympathy and the will to help those in need and trouble. Socially conscious he made an annual Christmas appeal for the poor of the parish and by the response to it assisted people without regard to denomination.

St Clement's was a "poor shipyard parish" for its members, loyal and generous as they were, had little of this world's goods and most of them depended on their livelihood in the shipyard, factories and foundries of Ballymacarrett.　None of these were in good state since war ended in 1945.　Things began to improve in the 1950s when the Stormont Government persuaded many industrialists to come to Northern Ireland to buildings provided for them.　They brought working conditions incomparably better than anything known before.

Fisher was an enthusiast for the English language which was somewhat incongruous, for his parishioners had a very limited vocabulary. It was said that his bed time reading was Chamber's Dictionary and I was to find that he had a love for good literature and a use of language unequalled by anyone I have ever met. Only occasionally did he get the chance to display his erudition in learned company. And on occasion he would be naughty in his use of words. I remember being with him at a meeting – not of the parish – when he criticised his hearers in words and phrases unknown to them. When they applauded him for what they thought he had said in commendation of them he asked me, "Did they understand what I said?" When I replied, "Not a word of it", he laughed gleefully.

Fisher was inordinately proud of his ancestry for he had family connections with those Fishers which included Admiral Lord Fisher of the Broke. When I asked was he a relation of Geoffrey Fisher, Archbishop of Canterbury, I got the brush off with, "Oh, no, he is one of the common Fishers." And he was an autocrat who believed that as rector of the parish his word should carry such force that only the grossly impertinent would question it. At my first vestry meeting he was having difficulty getting a matter agreed and as an argument began to develop he stood up and demanded, "Bow your heads." When they did he said the Grace and closed the meeting. Tapping me on the shoulder he said, "Come we're here long enough tonight." On the way from the room he whispered, "When we meet again they'll have calmed down." This kind of imperiousness would not be tolerated now, not only because vestries and parishioners are more articulate, but for the reason that his kind of clergyman has well nigh vanished from the scene.

While not many of Fisher's contemporaries would have acted as imperiously as he did several of them were remarkable characters. There were men like Louis Crooks, John Frazer, James Quinn, Cyril

Elliott, Charles Houston in our area and in other parts of Belfast there were Lyndon, Williams, Cooke, Breene, Lindsay, Maguire.

There, too, was the Bishop of Connor, Charles King Irwin, with his curt manner and economy of words. Many of his clergy received the briefest of correspondence from someone who used words as a miser spends money. A curate showed me a postcard from the bishop replying to two questions he had asked on a personal matter and a possible change of curacy and diocese. The card read "1) No. 2) No."

Canon Fisher was a good preacher with something of an actor's sense of the dramatic in speech and movement. On a sea cruise when his fellow travellers tried to guess his occupation the consensus opinion was that he must be a Shakespearian actor. Strength lay in his careful use of illustration and quotation. Regrettably he suffered from a bronchial condition which meant that he preached less often than he had done in other days. This meant that he had many guest preachers whom I had to replace in their churches. I came to know well several churches in Down and Dromore and Connor dioceses.

I was a short time in the parish when I was made aware of poison pen letters which had troubled it for some years. These were addressed to a few of my predecessors in the curacy and to curates in neighbouring parishes. The culprit was discovered in my time and by some good amateur detective work in which I was involved. Circumstances were such that no action was taken. A threat of disclosure with dire consequences ended a pernicious and irrational campaign.

I enjoyed my curacy of three years in St Clement's. My intention was to move at two years, the usual practice with a first curacy at the time, but I stayed longer on the plea of Canon Fisher who was contemplating retirement. Ellie and I with Norman who had been born on 7 July 1950 found the parishioners kindly and generous. The churchwardens at my ordination were Harry Echlin Neill and Tom McMurray. Neill, a commercial artist was also a fine landscape and portrait painter. He was always ready with a word of appreciation to the new curate. Tom McMurray, with his wife May, often acted as our babysitters and were our very good friends. McMurray was succeeded by Tom Rain, newsagent and later commercial traveller, who remained in that office for forty years. He had been a long serving member of the Diocesan Council and the General Synod and a Parochial Nominator. There were Church Lad's Brigade and Girl Guides' companies in the parish. I recall one incident with the boys which happened after a drill and games night. I had left the hall and reached the street when I felt I should go back to check that all was well, to find two seniors fighting. I broke up the fight, and fearing its consequences for the company, gathered the lads around me and after ensuring that the boxers would be friends again made all of them promise not to speak of what had happened, for Canon Fisher, the martinet, would close down the C.L.B for such a breach of discipline. The promise was made and kept. It was many years later that one of the company reminded me of the incident.

Tom Rain, as Sunday School Superintendant, persuaded me in my first few months to start a study class for the fourteen to eighteen year olds, a sort of post-confirmation group. It proved to be a worthwhile project as a contribution to the life of the Church. The class meeting on Sunday afternoons needed an organist. I got a reluctant player who after a couple of weeks advised me that Jim Drennan was "going to music" and would be a much better organist than he had proved to be. He was right Jim is a very good organist and has been organist and choirmaster of St Molua's, Stormont, for several years after a period in St Donard's, Bloomfield. Another of my St Clement's boys, Stanley Irvine, was the rector of the parish of Ballina in the West of Ireland.

It was as a curate in St Clement's that I joined the Loyal Orange Institution. I had been a member of a junior lodge as a boy and while I had retained an interest in the organisation I had not become a member of the Orange Order proper. I was "made an Orangeman" in LOL No. 428 of which Canon Fisher was chaplain, and on whose banner was a portrait of Canon Harding, sometime rector of Willowfield with which the lodge maintains a connection.

8

THE CHURCH AND ITS ORGANISATIONS

When I accepted the appointment to the neighbouring parish of Willowfield from John Frazer, rector, I had expressions of disapproval from several colleagues, Canon Fisher, among them who considered it wrong for me to go to another East Belfast parish when a change to a town or suburban one would have given me more in variety and experience. I thought they were wrong then and have not changed my mind with hindsight. I found Willowfield so different from St Clement's that I could hardly have made a better choice. The differences were not to be seen as meaning something of great importance, for the similarities in Irish Anglicanism far outweighed the differences. This was an Irish characteristic, for Anglicanism in other countries have many variations in worship patterns and procedures.

St Clement's was strong on the value and use of the liturgy. Canon Fisher maintained that a Church of Ireland clergyman should never be slovenly in his use of language for he had the Book of Common Prayer as a pattern for his usage of words and its communication of ideas. The care that was taken in the reading of services, the emphasis on articulation and pronunciation in praying, reading and preaching, was a constant persuasion on clergy and people to give of their best in whatever they had to do. I have always been grateful for the emphases of the rector and parishioners of my first appointment.

Willowfield had characteristics different to St Clement's because it was a much larger parish and it was an overseas missions minded church. Its support for the Bible Churchmen's Missionary Society was a large part of the giving of the people to the work and witness of the Church. And it gave support to several other societies and agencies whose commitment was to the growth of the Church and the betterment of people.

The most obvious enthusiasm in the parish came from the Christian Endeavour Society with its separate age groups catering for the younger and older in Bible study with the aim of building them up in their faith. The elaborate CE system meant that members were encouraged to think deeply in ordered fashion on spiritual and material matters and to express their thoughts on topics set for that purpose. The opportunity CE gave to members to speak at meetings proved to be a benefit to them in public speaking. It helped some of them to prepare for service at home and abroad as ministers and missionaries.

The benefits of CE were not to be questioned but it had the disadvantage common to all such organisations it could be self interested and self satisfied. The determination to support its own and the tendency to crowd together meant that it could be a church within the church, a pressure group roading the church in the direction it determined it should go.

The attitudes of Willowfield CE at times alienated other parishioners, the larger number of whom had no contact with it. Because they were not organised the CE element gained position and influence greater than was warranted by its numbers. Not that anything was done illegally, for the votes at generally crowded General Easter Vestry meetings were properly counted and elections duly declared. However I was shown a list authorised by the CE of the people it wanted to be elected to office when elections are supposed to be free and without pressure of any kind. The tactic meant that the CE and those whom they favoured provided the parochial nominators who had the responsibility of representing the parish at Boards of Patronage; so they effected the appointment of incumbents and ensured a succession of conservative evangelical rectors.

While some resentment was expressed at the activities of CE the parish was remarkably happy and the clergy were able to do their work unaffected by the Willowfield situation. That the parish had organisations which catered for those for whom CE had no attraction must have accounted for the good relations which I found when I joined the staff there.

The rector was John Frazer and my curate colleague W.O.R. Davies who in six months was to become an army chaplain. He was succeeded by Edward Hastings who was ordained for the parish in December 1953, but an illness a few days afterwards, kept him in his home or in a Dublin hospital until October 1954.

John Frazer was as remarkable a character as Willie Fisher but it would have been impossible to compare them as clergymen or men for that matter. Where Fisher was an idealist, fastidious even, with an old world charm Frazer was practical, outspoken even tactless on occasion. He loved jokes and told them repeatedly but the serious was never submerged in the frivolous and he administered his large parish with sensitivity, skill and enthusiasm. An aged man when I joined him he was less active than he had been in other days but his mind and memory were unimpaired.

Indeed memory was his most marked characteristic. He illustrated that when as a Bible expositor he quoted whole passages of scripture with comment verse by verse and always without notes. After many years listening to sermons and hearing preachers noted for their expository preaching I have found none like John Frazer of Willowfield. Among the clergy he was recognised as an able financier for he had managed to put both his parishes, St Michael's and Willowfield, on sound financial footing. Like Fisher he could be autocratic in his dealings with vestrymen, leaders of organisations and parishioners, and like Fisher he did not always have happy relations with his organists. Both men changed hymns before services, "*out of badness*" the organists said. It is possible the motive was to keep the organists aware of the fact that the incumbent should have the last word in the ordering of the worship of the Church.

When I went to Willowfield on 1 April 1952 I was to find need for other organisations to cater for young people large in number at the time. On 5 May 1953 fifty three, thirty girls and twenty three boys, were confirmed. A Boy's Brigade Company, 5th Belfast, was founded and I was fortunate to make the acquaintance of two deeply committed BB men, Norman and Tom Jeffers, when I officiated at a family funeral. They had been associated with the Cregagh Presbyterian Company while retaining a Willowfield Parish connection. With Norman as captain and Tom lieutenant the 5th was well launched. As Company Chaplain I had the responsibility of ordering the Bible Class, the first one on 27 September 1953 and I was acquainted again with the set text books of that most prolific Christian writer, William Barclay. The Jeffers were excellent officers and they remained in their posts for many years. As the Parish had a troop of Boy Scouts the BB, which catered for boys for whom Scouting had no attraction, was never a large one but the high quality of its work on the floor and for badges guaranteed its continuance.

I preached at the 25th anniversary service of the 5th on 30 September 1977 when the rector, David Hutchinson, former rector Harold Lowry, Gordon McMullan and John Gribben another former BB officer now ordained, took part. And I was honoured to be the Inspecting Officer at the 25th Anniversary Inspection and Display of the company on 14 April 1978. We were the guests at the anniversary dinner next evening when the speakers were the rector, Gordon McMullan, Tom Cromie (BB President) Tom and Norman Jeffers and John Clarke. Gordon was MC and in my speech I reminisced on the beginnings of the 5th and commented with pleasure on its successful past, and promising future.

9

RETURN OF THE GLORIOUS GAME

I was approached by a few young men aware of my interest in soccer to ask me to consider setting up a football club. When we called a meeting on 23 June 1953 the attendance showed that the project had merit. Again I was fortunate for Gordon McMullan was elected club secretary and by 29 July we had arranged a few friendly matches. Meetings were held on 4 and 17 August when it was decided to order soccer kits made possible by the grant of £25 from the Select Vestry. And on 5 September the club had its first kick-about. The first match at Ormeau Park was against the Castlereagh Laundry when we lost 7 goals to 2. I had the distinction of scoring the first goal for a Willowfield Parish team. We had a happier result in the second game against Railway United when we won 5 goals to 0. The team at the beginning was A. McBride, G. McMullan, E. Reid, G. Best, B. Blacoe, S and W. Thompson, J and T. Johnston, W. Hunter, S. Murphy, J. Carson, and J. Weir. Players who joined later were David Calderwood, V and E.

Hunter, J. Charles, A and S. Sherwin, J. McKeown, K. Allen, S. Kerry, R, Kane, J. Davidson.

From the beginning the club had a weekly meeting when more than soccer was discussed.

Application was made for membership of the Churches' League and Billy Hunter and I met with league officials on 30 July 1954 when the club was admitted. The first league match was away to St Donard's, Dundrum, when we were narrowly defeated 5 to 4 and I was injured for the first time ever on a football field. When I was examined by Dr. Gorman at his surgery on the Castlereagh Road and he had diagnosed severely pulled muscles in my right leg and added the advice, "Its either into goals or retirement for you." I decided I had had enough and played seriously no longer.

The club had made such progress that a second team had been registered on 28 August 1954. The firsts now played in black and white stripes, for the seconds had adopted the original red of the club. The firsts had their biggest win in the 1955/6 season when they defeated Monkstown away 9 – 0 and Winkie Thompson scored five goals. Shortly afterwards he signed for Linfield. Because I had encouraged the players to talk with me before making such a decision he came seeking advice before putting pen to paper. I did not try to dissuade him though his going would be a grievous loss to us but I pointed out that as he had thoroughly enjoyed his football with Willowfield he should know that if things did not work out with the Blues we would be delighted to have him back. His time with the Irish League club was short and he returned to Willowfield to play for the next twenty years and to score a pile of goals.

Willowfield Parish F.C had become a brotherhood in which lasting friendships were made. Incidentally the club had four sets of brothers – Billy, Victor and Eddie Hunter, Sammy and Winkie Thompson, John and Tommy Johnston, and Archie and Sam Sherwin. It developed a community consciousness so that at an annual Christmas party for senior citizens it entertained many guests.

It was expected of the players that they attend the Sunday afternoon Fellowship Class in Church, September to April. From the beginning we wanted it to be more than another football club. We take pride in the fact that of the original pool of players Gordon McMullan became the Bishop of Down and Dromore, Brian Blacoe rector of Annalong and Knocknamuckley, Jim Carson a Presbyterian minister, Jim Davidson a London City Missionary and David Calderwood a missionary with an American society. Others among them have been office bearers in the Church notably George Best, Winkie Thompson, Victor Hunter and Alan McBride.

Rt. Rev. Dr. Gordon McMullan
Bishop of Down and Dromore
1986-1997

While my office was club chairman I was also manager of the first team taking all managerial decisions. I have to add that no soccer club manager was ever better treated and supported by his officials and players. Playing pitches were always at a premium for junior clubs. We were fortunate to have "The Stadium" at Cregagh. It became our ground after Billy Hunter, as club secretary, and I had convinced the reluctant owner of the field that he would be rendering a great service to society if he granted our request. Mr and Mrs McKelvey became my very good friends and mugs of tea and home baked buns were my half-time refreshment on the call of the farmer at our home games.

Unfortunately my leaving the parish coincided with their plans to dispose of the land for industrial development and the club has had the use of several playing fields since those days.

Ellie and I were the guests of the Willowfield Parish F.C at a 15th anniversary service in the church on 21 April 1968. Gordon McMullan and Brian Blacoe read the service and Billy Hunter and Tom Jeffers the lessons. The soloist was Ivan Foster and I was the preacher. We had a most pleasing cuppa after the service when greetings were read from David Calderwood (USA) and Jim Davidson (London). We were guests again at the 21st anniversary party on 18 September 1974 and at a church service on the 22nd when Gordon McMullan preached and I dedicated gifts from the club to the Church.

The Willowfield Fellowship class was a bright, free-and-easy Sunday afternoon service originally for older teenagers and young adults but very soon it was attended by older people.

10

SUNDAY SCHOOL AND SUCH

A gain my introduction of a new venture came from the request of Sunday School teachers who wanted their pupils to stay under church influence after confirmation. The Church of Ireland is always aware of the loss of young people from church attendance and activities ironically after they have been confirmed into the membership of the Church.

The class opened in Church on 26 October 1952 and the fifty who attended that afternoon were soon to see their numbers grow until the average was nearer two hundred. Again I was fortunate in having the services of a talented organist, Miss Muriel Gough. As our accompanist to the many singers we had, she was most sensitive and helpful. Secretaries Mr and Mrs Bob Gallagher used their contact with singers to such good effect that every service had musical content extra to the class singing which was always an important feature. We had soloists, duettists, quartets and choirs, and because the singers were chosen with care all were well known and some were prizewinners at the Belfast Musical Festivals.

The class had a simple liturgy and only on a few occasions had we a visiting speaker. So that from September to April for four seasons I gave the addresses. We were proud of the camaraderie which developed among the members who included those who had other or no church connection. The church should welcome anyone who is interested enough to attend its services or organisations. Exclusivism does not square with the whosoever will of Jesus.

Among the most memorable class services were those carols and readings before Christmas and hymns and readings at Easter. While we never equalled the attendance of the first Fellowship Class Christmas service, 450, we had 270, 200 and 250 at the others. The Easter services, governed more by date and weather, had around 200 on each occasion. We had an annual social, well attended and much enjoyed.

Another memorable feature of my ministry in Willowfield was the annual Holy Week services. In 1953 I introduced "*Living Bible*" films on the life and ministry of Jesus and placed them in a setting of singings, prayers, readings and a talk of a few minutes. I was indebted to Robert Cordner, who used his film projector each evening after overcoming his reluctance to show pictures in which Jesus was portrayed by an actor. But the films were so true to the New Testament in location, speech and action and the actor so sensitive that he was contented to project them. My figures for the couple of years that we had this Holy Week format in the tennis pavilion which doubled as another parochial hall averaged 150.

The Willowfield Church Sunday services were an experience to be savoured. The large square nave, which may have been regarded as less beautiful than the more traditional cruciform shape of other churches, had its value as a preaching place. The Church had weaknesses which were noticeable, for the sanctuary and chancel, small and cramped, were out of proportion to the rest of the building. Attendances were good in the years I served there with large numbers at evening services.

These were the days before television and the many other distractions changed the attitudes of people to Sunday and church attendance. It was a privilege to serve in a parish where so much was happening involving so many people. The outreach of the church was impressive, with both the clergy and the laity working hand in hand.

It was Willowfield that provided Ellie, Norman and I with our first house. In St Clement's we had lived in apartments and in a flat in Templemore Avenue. The Select Vestry in Willowfield purchased 298 Woodstock Road beside the site of the new parish hall and with the tennis courts and pavilion behind us. We moved in on 28 October 1952 with the help of a few vestrymen. Housing was at a premium at that time particularly for those like us whose future lay elsewhere and where a house would be provided for us. Since 1949 we had searched for a house and experienced what house-hunters must have felt always, frustration and promises of help which produced nothing but kept hope alive for a while. There was a St Clement's parishioner who would have bought a small house which he would have rented to us but when we thought we had one a surveyor friend gave it a professional examination and warned us off. In another case we had made an offer to be advised after a few days that we were topped and the house was sold. After another few days the agent made contact to tell me the sale had fallen through. He offered to sell at the price he had accepted from the other bidder. We felt we were being conned and said "No thanks" to leave the man pleading his integrity. We were not impressed.

11

A COUNTRY PARISH

My appointment to the grouped parishes of Dromara and Garvaghy was on 30 April 1956 with the Institution on 21 June 1956. The interval was necessitated, for we were expecting our second child, Colin, who was born on 20 May 1956. Ellie had an especially difficult confinement. Colin and the daughter of Eddie and Mrs Hastings were duly baptized by John Frazer in Willowfield Church.

The Institution took place on a glorious summer evening and I was pleased to have present family and friends, parishioners from St Clement's and Willowfield, St Aidan's where I had been a Lay Reader and St Philip's, many of my clerical colleagues and neighbouring ministers with many members of the organisations to which I belonged.

When clergymen move from one parish to another their farewell services receive special attention. I was thrilled at mine on 17 June

1956 in Willowfield when the attendance was six hundred with another hundred at Ballarat Street Hall that evening. The hall had Sunday evening services taken by the clergy in turn, an afternoon Sunday School and was meeting place for a couple of organisations.

The clerical manpower situation in the Church of Ireland was very different in the 1950s from what it is now. And it remained so until the 1980s. In the Fifties there were many clergymen available for appointments and especially in the often preferred dioceses of Down and Dromore and Connor. While it was regarded as the thing not done, that is to apply to fill a vacancy no one doubted that overtures were made by clergymen for themselves or for others, sometimes with the help of influential laymen, to bring about an appointment. There were rectors whose curates received preferment because they used their influence to help them. The reverse was true in a case where a rector and curate were finding it a problem to work together. The rector met a dignitary of the diocese who enquired, "Is Mr Blank your curate?" He answered, "Yes and I'm sorry he is." A day or two later he knew the reason behind the question for the dignitary had been on his way to a Board of Patronage at which the curate's name was to be considered for the vacancy. Blank remained his curate for quite a while longer! Bishops were blamed for showing preferences, though there must have been times when those who made charges were speaking from emotion rather than evidence.

Much of the clerical dissatisfaction in the 1950s to 1970s came from appointments which were thought to be manipulated and a contradiction of the spirit of Christian vocation. If the impression I give of clergy being self interested and anxious about their prospects is seen as unbecoming to men in the ministry of the church it is because clergymen can be as practical and ambitious as others whose professions make lesser demands on them. And there have always been clergy who could have made more lucrative livings in another occupation. It was said of Archbishop Cosmo Gordon Lang that had he gone into business he would have been a merchant prince. The discontent over appointments reached its heights when at a meeting of the Down Clerical Society the decision was taken to send a "Round Robin" to the clergy inviting them to sign and by so doing register their protest about a few annoying elections. A few of us thought the method was wrong and suggested that the better way would be to make the bishop aware of the depth of feeling caused by decisions of Boards over which he had presided. The list went round, and while some signed without hesitation, there were those who gave reasons for refusing to do so which showed not disagreement with the complaints but fear of the career consequences to themselves.

The bishop when he learned of the "Round Robin" must have been discomfited by the fact that those who refused to sign were no happier with the situation than those who had put pen to paper.

The protest had its effect, for two appointments were cancelled. The one by withdrawal, the other by a Church of Ireland decision which prevented the acceptance of the incumbency.

A number of circumstances have contributed to the present position when clergymen are in short supply. The opportunities available to university graduates more numerous and varied is one of them. Others include the secularisation of our society and the diminished interest in religion. There is the earlier retirements of Church of Ireland clergymen. When I was ordained and for many years afterwards our clergy rarely retired and never of their own volition. This meant that there were incumbents of up to ninety years of age because the Church had a Widows and orphans Fund but no Retirement Fund. The other Protestant churches were different, arrangements were such that their ministers could retire in their mid sixties. It was the 1960s before a Pensions scheme was launched and it took several years, and the injection of large sums of money before pensions were at a reasonable level.

Improved clerical salaries are making it easier for men to prepare for retirement and the Church of Ireland Housing Association and the Church of Ireland Housing Trust have made their contributions to that end.

Looking back I find it almost unbelievable that we managed to live on the salary I received as curate and incumbent for many years. The kindness of a local shopkeeper in our Belfast years, the sympathy of the bank and mainly Ellie's excellent housekeeping made the impossible possible. Our situation was no different to most other clerical families. In those days, too, it was regarded as improper for the wife of a clergyman to be in business or profession. This attitude is long gone. Many clergy wives have their jobs which they manage to combine with housewifely chores and parish involvements. There appears to be a better understanding among parishioners now on the place of rectory ladies in our parishes.

Ellie always available for participation in church affairs and organisations enjoyed the sympathy and support of women and girls over the years. Most clergy wives are as deeply committed to the

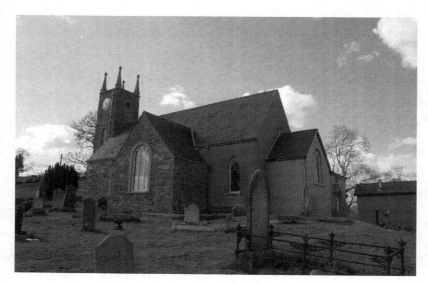
St. John's Parish Church, Dromara

Church as their husbands. Our indebtedness to them is not always adequately expressed.

The Institution of Dromara and Garvaghy started me on a much longer ministry there than I could have anticipated. Having only a passing acquaintance with country life we faced the future with some trepidation. We were to find and enjoy that remarkable friendliness which always characterised country folk. Our neighbours were invariably kind and considerate. We needed them when in that first Christmas we were without light and minus cooking facilities. They kept us going with hot water and they cooked our food while the storm lasted. We got to know a lot about Dromara winters in the years that followed, though never again were we unprepared for their snow and ice. The Church of Ireland Rowans and the Presbyterian McKnights were our saviours.

12

A RECTORY FOR A HOME

The rectory built in 1739 was in poor state when we came to it. Even though £1100 had been spent in the months prior to the summer of 1956 water and vermin were breaking and entering. It was clear that the vestries had two options to completely overhaul and remodel the house or to build a smaller one. The old Georgian rectory had an attraction for those parishioners who remembered it in better days but none was unaware of the problems it created in maintenance and running costs. The rectory was to be an item on the agenda of St John's Select Vestry for a few years.

On 3 January 1957 Denis O'D Hanna, the diocesan architect declared that the reconstruction and modernisation of the house was beyond the capacity of the parish and he suggested providing a plan for a new rectory. I sought the expert advice of valuer friends, Bob Cuddy and Fred Greer, on 4 January and they advised sell and build. On 8 January the Vestry decided to sell at a price sufficient to meet the cost of a replacement. The sale was put into the hands of our solicitor, Dr Henry Magennis and estate agent Eric Thompson (G. D. Martin, Lisburn). An advertisement appeared in The Belfast Telegraph, 24 May 1957. But if we thought the rectory business was progressing satisfactorily we soon discovered that there were those who felt the rectory should not be sold.

At a congregational meeting on 24 February 1958, the Rural Dean, R.W. Kilpatrick being present, the spokesman for the group, John E. Bailey, MP, so influenced those present that a decision by vote was taken to keep and improve the house. What appeared to be a hard and fast decision was rescinded when at the next Vestry meeting on 10 June I presented an estimate from Blain Bros, Saintfield builders, on the cost involved in making the house as it should be. A new decision was taken to sell and build. Bids began to be made for the rectory and glebe of 32 acres. Because I had a conscience about selling off land, a continuously valuable commodity, I took advice from Mr Sherwood, county surveyor and much committed churchman and we marked out a division of the land which would mean we could sell the house and the gardens and a small field, total about seven acres, while retaining the remainder of the glebe. When an advert appeared with this change bids were for the part and not for the whole. As the Diocesan Council on 24 September 1958 had advised sell or repair properly, the Select Vestry on 27 November with church warden, Robert Thompson, in the chair sold the property to Lt.-Col F. M. Cunningham. A site in our own land was chosen for the new rectory on 5 August 1959. The Dromara representatives were John Jess, James Pollock, Sam Elliott and George Bell and for Garvaghy William Spiers, Fred McClughan and Sidney Kerr. Present was the builder Pharis Carlisle, Annahilt. Building began on 24 August 1959.

The Long Family outside the Rectory

As a family we benefited from the generosity of mill owner, George Ervine, Waringsford, who loaned us a newly refurbished house at Waringsford, for the period of our leaving Dromara Rectory until the new house was built. We moved there on 26 November 1959 to establish a lasting friendship with the whole Ervine family. When after fourteen months two Dromara Vestry men asked George Ervine for the rent account they were told that the arrangement for his house had been between him and me and he would talk with me on the matter. In the event our good Presbyterian friend would only take a few pounds as a nominal payment. In effect the letting was a gift to the Longs. Our family had grown by the birth of our third son, Mervyn, on 18 July 1958.

13

HALL OF FAME

Our first new parish building was not the rectory but a parish hall. Dromara parishioners had long wanted a hall of their own. They had been indebted to Second Dromara Church and the Orange Lodge for the use of their buildings for any social event. When we arrived there were plans for a hall and £1000 had been raised for a hall fund. Unfortunately the state of Church funds were such that the money had been needed to augment them.

After my negotiations with Barbour Simpson, Solicitors, Lisburn, we managed to purchase a site near the Church from the Hunter Family for a nominal £100. Vestryman and local builder, Sam Hunter, prepared plans for a hall which were accepted at a vestry meeting on 22 January 1957. The arrangement was that we would supply all materials, clear the site and lay the foundations by voluntary labour. Nothing would have been possible in the project had not John Jess and I had a meeting with James McCormick, builders' supplier, Ballynahinch. We trysted with him for what he could supply with payment to be made as we had the money to pay. Mr McCormick always insisted that he should be paid after our other suppliers.

The site was cleared on 4 May 1957 and Voluntary work began on 6 May. The foundations were laid by 1 June 1957. The builders began on 13 June and the foundation stone ceremony was on 5 July when Mrs J. H. McCormick laid the stone and Canon John Barry, Hillsborough, dedicated it.

The official opening was on 9 November 1957 by John E. Bailey, MP., for West Down, in the absence through illness of the Governor of Northern Ireland, Lord Wakehurst, and the dedication was by the Bishop, F. J. Mitchell. There was a guard of honour of Boy's Brigade and Girl's Brigade. And the very large attendance included clerical colleagues and special guests the Lord Clanwilliam, D. L. and the Rev. W. J. Gregg.

The commodious hall was to be much used by our own and community organisations for special events. None of them failed to use St John's Hall.

The parish organisations Ladies Guild, BB, GB were joined by a newly founded Indoor Bowling Club and later badminton and youth clubs were added. Soon there was a weekly day centre for senior citizens. The BB first met in the rectory on 19 September 1956 with the first enrolment on 13 January 1957. The GB had its first night in the rectory on 30 November 1957. The Ladies Guild had been active for several years to become a branch of the Mother's Union in 1958. The bowling club opened with a match versus the Magheradroll club on 3 December 1957. Twelve would be bowlers had been shown something of the game when they visited the Willowfield club on 28 October 1957. The club flourished and I became the organiser of many bowls tournaments.

There were many money raising events for the Hall Fund – guest teas, concerts, plays and weekly parties with bands, games and dances. These were the days when musicians could be engaged for a few pounds and good artists for little more. And we introduced pantomimes to the area with the Fernagh Players, Rathcoole, Belfast, in Dromara and the Cregagh Players, Belfast, in Garvaghy. The first of them was in Dromara on 24 January 1958 and in Garvaghy 19 January 1963. They were productions eagerly looked forward to by most appreciative audiences which filled to overflowing St John's Hall and Garvaghy Presbyterian Church Hall. There were seven pantos in Dromara and two in Garvaghy. The Festival of Fashion organised by Councillor Ben Horan, 23, 24 March 1961 was something never to be forgotten. It was magnificent and opened on the first night by Lady Dunleath and on the second by Mrs Dorcas Dickson, Dromore.

The hall was paid off in a few years for every parishioner played a part. They contributed in collections which meant much door to door visiting for me on an errand I was never to repeat. A Brick Card scheme produced a sizable sum from friends of parishioners.

14

ONE MOMENTOUS YEAR

We were also making changes in the Churches. Garvaghy installed an electronic Miller organ which was dedicated by the Dean of Dromore, Dr. Orr, on 16 June 1957. The organ in Dromara, a fine two-manual pipe organ, was electrified and restored by the Irish Organ Company with a re-dedication by the Archdeacon of Down, George Quin.

The volume of work done in the parishes in the first year of my incumbency received the attention of Cromlyn in The Church of Ireland Gazette and mentioned in the Diocesan Synod of 27 May 1958. I wrote a booklet *One Momentous Year* published on 21 February 1958 to chronicle what had been done.

Heavy expenditure meant that we were constantly concerned about cash flow. That in mind I brought Mr Mahouey of the Wells Organisation to talk to the Select Vestry of St John's on Christian Stewardship on 30 May 1958 and 9 January 1959 without result. It was 1985 before we had a most successful Stewardship Campaign under the guidance of the Church of Ireland Stewardship Office.

It is incumbent on me to write specifically of the Church of Ireland and of my life long commitment to it.

In the 1930's it was numerically strong. Church attendance, seen by critics as a Sunday habit "the done thing," was for many meaningful and satisfying with its emphases on the worship of God, the sharing together in the public expression of faith, the ministry of the Word and the sacraments of the Gospel.

The services were according to the Rites and Ceremonies of the Church of Ireland and with the Book of Common Prayer. Preaching was important for the sermon had value as a teaching medium, integral to the public presentation of the faith, persuasion to spiritual growth and to character and conduct consonant with it.

There were church organisations with purposes in teaching, learning and recreation; for personal improvement, shared experiences and the development of friendships.

The outreach of the Church was needed to help many in days with unemployment rife, and the poverty, distress and disease that went with it. People were helped with education, encouraged to belief in themselves and support for them to face their problems and to progress in spite of them.

There were more clergy then whose sense of vocation had to be strong for pay was poor and accommodation little better. They got about on foot or bike or by tram, bus and train.

The standard of living for people only changed when the Thirties ended, for with the war there was work in aircraft factories and shipyard. Improved circumstances with money helped the economy to take better shape with benefits for everyone.

Remarkably the improvements adversely affected the Church for other interests were developed and attitudes changed. They did not place a high valuation on Church attendance and Sunday for many was church-less.

Changes in society have been so revolutionary that to look back is to recognise the chasmic gulf between what was a religious society and the secular one of today.

There were mental and physical prohibitions of the past where now there are allowances, acceptances, permissiveness, and in the Church there are those deeply committed to the beliefs of the centuries enshrined in Scripture, the 39 Articles of Religion, the Creeds and Prayer Book, there are others who refuse to be bound by "restrictions." They think and do what conscience permits and faith allows. This attitude has had serious repercussions in the Church for its services vary so much from what was the norm that they bear little resemblance to the liturgical patterns of the past while there is a sameness with churches of other denominations of very different origins and attitudes. The effects are so well known they need no describing here.

It is reprehensible that Church of Ireland clergy, leaders of change, ignore the vows and promises of their ordination and disobey the rules and regulations of the church by which they receive their commission and care.

Autocratic leadership lacking the consent of the people has failure built in to it. The refusal to recognise the ethos of the Church by ignoring its Constitutions and Canons Ecclesiastical is to be condemned as dishonourable, dishonest and hypocritical. If change is necessary it should come by decisions of General Synod for

> "The General Synod is the supreme legislating authority and can make laws which affect the whole church. It is the only body which can alter the worship and doctrine of the Church. Only the General Synod can express the opinion of the Church of Ireland." *A Look at the Church of Ireland* (Diocese of Down and Dromore, 1992.)

The Church must study the effects of indiscipline and act in response to it. It is not a democracy but it operates best when decisions are taken for the whole church by the whole church.

The episcopate is of the essence of Anglicanism. Respect for its bishops has been a feature of the Church of Ireland. A recent reason could be they avoided controversies which grievously affect other Anglican churches whose bishops are seen to be unorthodox in theology, liberal in morality and partial in politics. Careful to acknowledge the attitudes of the members has meant that Irish Anglicanism is more conservative than elsewhere.

Questions were asked on Episcopal oversight when parishioners suffer from the deemed faults of a pastor whose ministry alienates them from their church and appeals to the bishop has had no effect. It appears then that bishops were unable to discipline clergy.

But there were bishops whose opinions and decisions left no-one in doubt on what they wanted done in any situation. J.A.F. Gregg was the Primate of whom it was said, "No-one speaks for the Church of Ireland until Gregg does." He was known to me as an apologist for the Reformed Faith in the Controversy over Roman Catholicism. And Charles King Irwin, Connor, whose communications were in few words, concise, pungent and demanding affirmative response. Another was Anthony Hanson, Clogher, who castigated clergy for lack of scholarship and leadership and laity for sectarianism, stultifying and repressive in a world needing release from mental and physical dogmatism and domination.

15

TRADITIONAL ROUTES

We differ from other churches in how we elect or appoint bishops and how we place clergy in parishes. Naming candidates and reporting on voting figures in an Electoral College for a bishop or a Board of Patronage for a parish is not our way. But transparency must be preferable. There is no need for secrecy. It is a nonsense to expect participants not to divulge what happens at such meetings, even when they sign not to tell. People being what they are, how do you prevent a leak? .

It is disconcerting to be told "we always did it that way" when asked why we do things in a certain fashion.

We are amazed, though, by the church's use of computers, the machines are integral to its work and witness when we struggled through with the simple means of communication they replaced.

There is simplicity in the kind of ministry summed up in the following advice given to an ordinand from Canon McQuaid:

> "You will need three books, a Bible, a prayer book and a visiting book. Read your Bible, say your prayers and visit your people. What is primary is your personal relationship to God and to your people." *Mark of Protest* (Dublin: Gill & Macmillan, 1993).

It is something most regretful that the Church, especially in the urban situation, has lost the so called working class. It is seen on the evidence as middle class and a cold place for the others whose status in society is different. Their loss to the church is a weakening of its work and witness so obviously that it cannot be questioned.

How to face up to the realities of life today is the perpetual problem. To diagnose the illnesses of our society is easier than to provide cures for them. The responsibility on the church is to continue to give the people the Gospel and to ensure that the Christian voice is heard, loud and clear, on everything that matters to them.

The ideal would be to speak with one mind and a single voice. The reality is that we differ on so much, people are confused and the Church is ignored with its values lost when they are always needed.

The Church! What of the future? Prospects are not good. It suffers from peoples disengagement from organisations where the complaint is, many losses few gains. A reason is that sons and daughters do not follow in train as their parents and grandparents did. Life for them is panoramoric, not static. Attractions multiply and choices are numerous.

They are freed from the restrictions of heritage and tradition. But without growth value and influence diminishes and weakness precedes closure. There were churches once alive, strong and satisfying to their numbers and highly regarded and much used by communities. They went that way.

This is the negative. There are positives in Church growth and the maintenance of work and witness effective in our often alien environment. The Church has its bright side. There are churches where caring and sharing make for a fellowship which has the faith ingrained in a togetherness in pursuit of their commission to bring people to faith in Christ and the faithful to a deepening of their spiritual experiences.

I am Church of Ireland by conviction and commitment. A primary reason is a high valuation on the liturgy of the Church; the literary excellence of its language, precise, pungent, purposeful; the dignity and discipline of a diet of worship with the blend of word, music and song and the constant use of Holy Scripture as its basic element.

16

LOCATION, LOCATION, LOCATION

The Dromara and Garvaghy hills are often a snow and ice hazard in winter. In these conditions on Sundays I had to weigh down the car with passengers sometimes and often with a boot full of cement blocks. I used a borrowed tractor from parishioner Lindsay Fee and with co-driver Sidney McKnight. I managed to keep my promise to conduct a Sunday service in Garvaghy Church until in February 1985 within sight of retirement the five miles journey proved to be impossible. On "snow Sundays" there were only two or three who gathered together in the Church in the heart of the hills. And after heavy snow there were floods, and places that held the water. Occasionally that meant taking off shoes and socks and rolling up trousers to push a stalled car out of the deep. Much of this kind of trouble was in my earlier years, improved road services helped to minimise the hazards latterly.

Dromara, a small village with a large, well populated hinter land and many smaller hamlets in a five mile radius, was largely dependent on agriculture. In 1956 the area was trying to emerge from relative obscurity. It had been off the railway tract. When the towns around lost their trains and buses were substituted, Dromara was made more equal with its neighbours. Marked progress had been made in the education of young people. Their parents, often highly intelligent were denied such opportunities. The availability of advanced education at eleven plus in grammar and secondary schools and technical colleges had opened up a new world to children who were being bused to schools and colleges in Lisburn, Ballynahinch, Banbridge, Dromore and Belfast.

The beneficiaries after the revolutionary changes in education were moving out to become professionals in education, medicine and law and in business and industry at every level. This meant marked changes in the population and greater movement of people than had been known previously. Many released by education and the opportunities it brought them were leaving to live nearer their places of employment. Others who commuted from home were becoming fewer and the full family more tenuous. It was many years before the trend reversed to an extent and when people viewed the country as more desirable than city or town. The influence of the motor car very limited in the Fifties was to be very significant later.

Until the end of the Forties Dromara men and boys had found employment in Dodds' flax mill and the women and girls in shops and sewing factories in the towns around.

In the Fifties the flax mill was gone and work was very scarce. The employment position was only mitigated because of the willingness of people to travel distances to work. For many of them that meant a lower standard of living than their work mates for their wages were reduced by the cost of travel.

Public representatives made overtures on behalf of Dromara to the Minister of Commerce and to the several businesses which were being persuaded to come to Ulster. Sam Magowan, MP for Iveagh with his lifelong knowledge of the area tried hard to persuade those with influence to provide work there. They were unmoved for a reason made clear when Tom Murphy and I were received by Lord Glentoran, Minister of Commerce, as representatives of the Town Committee on the work errand. He told us that the pool of labour in the Dromara area was so small relative to other needy areas that industrial development was not to be expected. Our contention that the labour pool was small because so many reluctant workers had to find their livelihoods elsewhere was not treated with the seriousness we thought it deserved. Much was made of the fact that of the number of those signing on the dole, some were 'unemployables' who were incapable of holding down a job.

Years later Dr. Eddie Rea came to Dromara with a vision of a specialist party plan children's clothing factory. He began his business in lofts and sheds before the fine factory of Elizabeth Alexandra – the names of his two young daughters – was built. He was to prove his ability and to make real his dream for the firm provided employment for a few hundred women and girls.

The Town Committee was founded in 1958 to plead the case of Dromara for it had been neglected in the provision of social and recreational facilities. There was a need for housing and better water and sewage amenities, road improvements and work of course. The committee with the local GP, Dr. William McBride, as chairman had some successes. It must be added though that the local Ulster Unionist Party branch had been pushing MPs and councillors to help Dromara and the earliest improvements at that time were due to them. When the Town Committee came into being a few of the unionists were among its most enthusiastic members. It was well into the Sixties before many of the sought for improvements came.

The economy of the country had showed such improvement that the number of cars and the improvement of housing were the tangible evidence of better days. The farmers were doing so well that all around were rebuilt farm houses and new ones for their families. Long before I left Dromara the changes could be described as incredible.

In our own case we had to suffer an inconvenience to do with water. When we built the new rectory it was on the understanding that we would have a mains water supply. When the house was ready for occupation the promise had not been kept and we took the forehardy decision to move in and to use a five hundred gallon tank to hold water which with the help of a small but powerful engine would be fed into the system. Drinking water would be taken from a well in our neighbour's garden. We were hurt and angry when the mains water came to find that the pipes stopped a few hundred yards from our house. Especially so when I had petitioned for water on the road since 1956 and my arrival in Dromara. The trouble arose from a misunderstanding on the location of the new house, for the council officers had assumed that it was sited between the old rectory and the village whereas it was on the upper side of the glebe lands.

We got the water but before the contractors came back to do the job we had nearly emptied the well and reduced the level of the Lagan as we filled the tank several times a week. Our neighbouring farmer parishioner, Lindsay Fee, was always available with his tractor to keep the tank filled.

You cannot have a large tank of water and young fellows playing around and not have accidents. Norman with his pals playing at balancing on the rim of the tank fell in. With the help of his friends he scrambled out and before he could be chastised for dangerous escapade I had chased his companions away. As I recall the incident I am reminded of a ducking I had when answering the call of a parishioner on the opposite hill. I chose to go by the fields across the valley to reach the house. It meant crossing narrow estuary of the Lagan which rises in the Dromara mountains. The leap had been easy in the past but there had been some heavy rain and the banks were slippery. I discovered that when I jumped and failing to get a foot hold I found myself in the deep water. Scrambling out on our side of the stream and drifting water I trudged the hill to home chagrined to find Norman, Colin, Mervyn and their friends waiting to "sympathise" with me. It seems that Norman told them not to laugh for if they did I would kill them. They did later and at every remembrance, and often since.

In the same bit of river one day I found a sheep in distress trying to scramble out to land to hear a voice say "give it a push it will come out all right." I saw no-one and did not recognise the voice. I am none the wiser as to the identity of him who spoke on the day I rescued a sheep from the water.

17

AMIDST THE PRESBYTERY

I was made aware on my arrival in Dromara that the area was predominately Presbyterian with five churches (one Reformed) all of them larger than our grouped parishes with their two churches. The good relationships that existed between us and our neighbours was continued happily through our years there. Thinking back on my incumbency it appears I was the immovable object. I stayed while most of those I travelled with went their several ways. The Presbyterian Churches had these changes: Ministers - First Dromara, William Wilson, Ronnie Wilson, Andy McComb and Frank McKeown; Second Dromara, Ernie Porter, Jack Bridgett, James Johnston and Jim Mattison; Garvaghy, Ivan McKnight and Andy Todd who had a ministry longer than mine; Drumlough, William Copes, Billy Grey and Scott Martin. The Reformed Church's two ministers were Renwick Wright and Robert Hanna and the Roman Catholic Church had Michael McDonald, Michael O'Rourke and Bernard Treanor.

My neighbouring Church of Ireland parishes had clergy going and coming, too. Magherahamlet, Cecil Thornton, Terry Sullivan, Victor McKeon and Eric Kingston; Annahilt, Ernie Clayton, Bill Harris, Tom McAuley, Jack Ferguson and Eric Kingston; Ballynahinch, Leslie Walker, Jack Shearer, Dick Morris, Cecil Cooper and Warren Russell; Dromore, Bob Kilpatrick, Ernie Clayton and Billy Neill; Drumgooland, Harold Lowry, Billy Hall, Hammy Lecky, Bob Rudd, Billy Neill, John McKigney and Robert Jones.

It was hardly surprising then that when a postman had to deliver a letter from America addressed to the Lord Mayor, City of Dromara, Ireland, it was passed on to me. As I had been sworn in as a magistrate in 1968 perhaps that made the decision the more understandable.

I could have moved from Dromara on several occasions, I even had approaches from Canada and the USA, but the country and its people with the freedoms I had to follow my other interests accounted for my willingness to stay. Dromara Church had known one very long incumbency. H. Echlin Boyd became rector at forty and was still in office when he died aged ninety-four. His brother Charles was rector of Magheradroll, Ballynahinch for fifty-six years. A curate of Magherahamlet, the Rev. George Bellet, in a history of that area wrote of the poor relationship between them "they never spoke to one another." Their father was a rector of Rathfriland and a translator of the works of Gabrielle Dante.

The snow of 1963 meant that in Dromara we were literally snowed in for a week 5 to 12 February. That was when Dr. W. S. McBride was taken by helicopter to tend a very sick patient up in the hills. He refused to be known afterwards as "the flying doctor." The roads were finally opened by gangs of men shovelling a way through. The lesson of 1963 must have been learned for there was no repeat of such a situation. The ready availability of snow clearing machinery has meant that roads have been kept passable.

The memory of my predecessor, the Rev. Stanhope S. Squires, was honoured when a headstone and grave surround was dedicated at a memorial service in St John's Church by his friend Herbert Frizell in January 1958.

Times of Sunday services were a problem when I arrived in the parishes. They alternated 11.30 and 3.30 and efforts had been made to regularise a service time for each Sunday. Dromara parishioners were unhappy with afternoon services and Garvaghy would not be satisfied only with them. After experimenting with times it was agreed that from 2 August 1959 Garvaghy's service would be at 10.45am and Dromara's at 12 noon and this agreement was kept thereafter.

18

CATCH THE PIGEON

My interest in the several varieties of pigeons began in childhood when a Bangor uncle showed me his loft and birds. Bangor was excited when his brother had the winner of the six hundred miles race from Les Sables in France in 1931. The bird flew the distance in fourteen hours, an incredible performance which was not equalled until many years later. Indeed Les Sables as a race point was abandoned for a long time on the ground that the distance with the hazards on the route was too much to ask of Irish pigeons.

My perplexing problem remains, "How is it possible for a homing pigeon to fly long distances at speed over land and sea often to a tiny loft in a back yard?" "And how did some pigeon fanciers produce a family of birds whose performances in long distance races earned them a reputation in the pigeon racing world?" One of them was Belfast man Billy Locke whose back yard shed was called 'The Elizabeth Lofts' from the street in which he lived off the Grosvenor Road. Many years after his death his strain of pigeons were still in demand. It is a fact that the racing pigeon is among the most valuable livestock in the world. The record prize for a champion bird several years ago was £72,000. The popularity of the sport world wide is amazing. In Belgium, the original home of the racing pigeon, fanciers have their homes built with an adapted roof space to accommodate a loft of birds. The size of the sport is emphasised in the weekly publication of two papers The Racing Pigeon and The British Homing World, two monthlies lavishly illustrated in colour and two Year Book/Diaries.

It was after attending a pigeon show, the Old Comrades, with its proceeds for the Great Ormond Street Children's Hospital, London, that I had a strange experience. Because I had to leave for college in Harrow before the show ended in the Royal Horticultural Hall I found myself in the street wondering about how to turn for the underground station. I turned right and after a moment or two doubted my decision. To my relief a man crossed the road near me and I asked him, "Could you tell me the way to Victoria underground station?" He smiled and said "I could and the way to Great Victoria Street Station in Belfast!" Of London's millions I had asked the way of a Lurgan man long domiciled in England, a trade union official and a communist from Stoke Newington. The coincidence was the more strange when he discovered that he could be distantly related to my wife. He was a Ferris too. My interest in pigeons showed in my writings. The articles appeared in Ireland's Saturday Night and I did talks on pigeons on BBC radio which had a talks department at the time. My producers were H.G. Fleet, John Boyd and John Body and the live broadcasts were 1946 to 1948; recorded programmes were hardly known then.

In 1942 I published a booklet *The Irish Pigeon Keeper* which had articles by well known fanciers. Out of it came an invitation to contribute regularly to an American monthly *The Pigeon Loft* whose publisher was Professor Carl Naether, Southern California University. The magazine made me break new ground for its main concentration was on breeds other than racing pigeons. I wrote about the Brunner Pouters of William McMillan of the Ulster Menu Company. These pigeons have long legs, light bodied frames and a blown out crop. They were of particular interest to Carl Naether and his readers who were better acquainted with Pigmy pouters whose crop was differently inflated. I got to know about bald pates, fantails, tumblers and horsemen, and fanciers who kept them like Mr Abernethy, the optician of Donegal Square South and Mr Fair, Rosetta House.

I already knew something of high flying tipplers for they were kept in many parts of the city. Much smaller than the racing pigeon and speckled coloured, they flew in competitions in kits of uneven number for up to fifteen hours none stop circling high above their lofts. I got to know one family whose men were very successful pigeon fanciers, for I had to make several visits to their North Queen Street home. On my last visit the three men and their sister left me to the door. Pat said to me, "Before you go I must tell you that we have been making guesses about you. We know you're not one of us and we think you are a student for the Protestant church. Could we be right?" When I told the Catholic people that they were, Mike surprised me when he said, "Now that we know that we want you to know that if we can do anything to help you we'll do it" and Pat added, "We'll sell birds or run a show or a competition if you will take what money we raise." When I assured them that I had what would see me through it was in the realization that words are not always adequate to reflect one's feelings.

I edited Jack Kilpatrick's still selling *The Thoroughbred Racing Pigeon* in 1948.

I also had an occasional article on pigeons in different publications. I wrote a few for The Racing Pigeon, 'The Same only Different' was about my early experiences of the sport and was published on 24th December 1970. Other articles appeared in The Mourne Observer and The Newtownards Chronicle. I have had little contact with the pigeon fraternity for many years. Occasionally I meet up with a few fancier friends and a nephew, Samuel Duke, is among the keenest of them.

19

CHARACTERISTICS OF WRITING

It must be obvious to anyone who reads what I write; that the written word has been a lifelong enthusiasm of mine. What is often most impressive in communication, person to person, people to people, is the use of it to enlighten, educate, enthuse and entertain others by the use of words, phrases and ideas that stimulate thinking on what is of consequence to us. The spoken word, however impressive, and the speaker, articulate, is "wind past the ears." Not much of what is said or spoken has permanence and only, at best, when the listener records what he hears, whereas the written word has a permanence, a continuing usefulness regardless of time - "words are pegs to hang ideas on."

Christians are the people of the book and that legacy of the written word is the gift we use constantly and profitably. The Bible and the literature it produces are integral to our thinking about life and its meaning for us.

My interest in writing came early. I have always done my thinking, in depth, with the help of pencil or pen, convinced of the value of writing to reader and writer. There is the pressure to say something when I feel something merits mention and comment. It is a matter of writing because I have a thought worth sharing. My writing has been a useful aid to ministry, and for long a continuance of ministry. It is a privilege and responsibility to address oneself to many readers, an attempt to reach and influence people who would not otherwise be touched.

I am not a provocative writer but an essayist. It is never my purpose to encourage controversy or to elicit negative reactions to what I write. I try to be helpful to people with their thinking on matters of consequence to me and of concern to them.

I invite the reader to "Think on these things" and to consider what is said if it is meaningful to them in their thinking on what merits attention and perhaps elucidation. We are reminded with Piet Jourbert that "Words, like glass, darken whatever they do not help us to see." The writer makes a personal contribution to the subject on which he writes. And what is written should have sincerity, simplicity and clarity. The reader must be able to understand what he is reading. If he has to wrestle with the meaning of words he is being offered something uncooked and inedible. It is imperative that facts should be verified and used with care.

I have written on subjects theological, philosophical, historical, practical and recreational and profiles of people, some famous persons, and others little known beyond their own village or town. All of them made their contribution, little or much, to the sum of the knowledge and the value of life.

To write means to read. My indebtedness to very many authors is readily acknowledged and illustrated in my use of questions from their works. The treasure trove of literature has given me an experience of inestimable value on very many subjects. While much of my reading is serious and purposeful there is also the trivial and escapist stuff to lighten the load.

The ministry of the church entailed a concentration on the faith, and writing devotional essays was integral to that. They appeared in some publications and in a book *Think on these things* (Schomberg Press, 2006). There is always the recognition that the Bible speaks for itself as God's ordinary means of conversation with us. The Christian writer has the duty to be true to Christ in what he writes, and always there must be the intention to see things from a Christian perspective. There is Christian thinking on everything that matters to people and often a biblical contribution to it.

I agree with Jourbert: "We should always keep a corner of our heads open and free, that we may make room for the opinions of our friends. Let us have heart and head hospitality" and with Samuel Zwemer thinking of the power of the printed page wrote: "No other agency can penetrate so deeply, abide so persistently and influence so irrestibly as the printed page."

My absorbing life long interest has been writing. It has meant being published frequently since my youth. The material has been varied, general and religious. The number of manuscripts has reached many hundreds. Because I have always believed that history is biography I have written a large number of profiles of varied lengths with subjects – Bishops Jeremy Taylor, Thomas Percy and Richard Mant, Archbishop William Alexander; the Reformers, Luther, Zwingli, Tyndale, Wyclif, Cranmer, Ridley and Latimer; the evangelists, Wesley, Whitefield; the Irish Presbyterians Hugh Hanna and W.P. Nicholson. There was *Men of America* for 1976 – Washington, Jefferson, Lincoln and Mark Twain; and hymn writers in a The Mourne Observer series in the years 1983 to 1989. Local personalities were featured in local papers from 1970.

I wrote and published as The Slieve Croob Press a number of booklets and included were *A Short History of the Parish of Dromara* (1979) and *A Short History of the Church of Ireland* (1979). Those on Unionism and Orangeism are mentioned elsewhere.

I authored a number of folders published by the Church of Ireland Temperance Board later to be incorporated in the Board for Social Responsibility (N.I.). They were on ethical and community problems – *Careful as you go*, *The Runaway from Reality*, *Hold your tongue*, *Freedom and Responsibility* and *What about Justice?* B.S.R. made use of my study on *Abortion* written in 1967.

I co-edited The Church Magazine of the Diocese of Down and Dromore and the essay in the Down and Dromore and Connor Home Mission's annual report to diocesan synods was mine until 1990 when I resigned the secretaryship. They generally produced lively debate from the floor of these assemblies. The committee published my folder *Personal Evangelism* for the synods of 1983.

And I was the Dromara Correspondent for local newspapers from August 1956 until October 1985 and contributor to The Church of Ireland Gazette for many years. My work has appeared in several publications in Britain and abroad.

Writing has allowed me to continue my ministry free from commitments integral to pastoralia in all its aspects. I value the opportunity I have of perpetuating the Christian message by means of the written word. And for reason that a single devotional article in one newspaper has a potential readership of 40,000, another of 15,000, and similar figures when I present a Christian perspective on political, religious and ethical matters of consequence to the everyday living of people in modern societies, locally, nationally, and internationally. It is most gratifying to reread in journals elsewhere and far away when editors think articles worthy of reproduction in their publications.

20

THE WORK OF OTHERS

I am sure that whatever happens in a ministry the relationship of minister and people is the important thing. I have always admired the loyalty, generosity and sympathy of church people. Differences are generally on the less important issues of church's life, people being as they are with freedom of speech and action, others are to be expected and welcomed. It is after shared thinking, discussion and debate that good decisions are made. The support of parishioners is an absolute essential if progress is to be made in and by the Church.

Because parishioners generally agree with decisions made by their clergy and elected officials it is most desirable to have the participation in administration of the most able people. I have appreciated and admired contributions of parishioners who in spiritual and material matters have worked ceaselessly for the church and the community it serves. Churchwardens, Vestry members, organists, choirs, Sunday

School teachers and leaders of organisations. The Church is fortunate when it has those who put their skill and experience freely at its service. We had such people in our grouped parishes and one Dromara man who stood out for the quality and quantity of his craftsmanship was Sam Elliott. The jobs he tackled and completed sometimes single handedly as carpenter and builder saved Dromara Church many thousands of pounds. A couple of examples were the plastering and floor strengthening of the floors of the interior of the tower and the installation of extra pews. They came to us as the gift of St Jude's, Ballynafeigh brought by a van driver Angus Kingham, Robert Thompson, Sam Elliott and the rector. Sam had the true tradesman's pride in his work. My "That looks well, Sam" often received the response "Oh, no, it still needs some work to make it right."

John Jess had been responsible for taking the lead in much of the voluntary labour which characterised parish attitudes to the maintenance and expansion of the church's property. His strength lay in his ability to encourage others to get involved. It is to their credit that they respond so readily.

We had the advantage of the sterling services of Church Treasurer Millar Kenny in his capacities as the teller of our money, confident advisor; always wise and totally dependable. He remained in his office until I retired.

I should add that I was singularly fortunate in having with me men and women like this in their loyalty and devotion to Christ and the Church.

It is extraordinary that in my ministry in Dromara I had two treasurers, James Pollock and Millar Kenny, two Rector's Churchwardens, Robert

Thompson and Ernest Jess; two Glebe Wardens, Robert Hart and Howard Jess. When James Pollock resigned as Church organist after sixty years Maureen Jess took his place and remained in that post with a short break when she left Dromara to live elsewhere. John Bailey proved to be a most able organist and choir master until Maureen returned and retired in 2007. In Garvaghy church Sydney Kerr was secretary and treasurer throughout my incumbency. Sydney had the parish in his heart and he served it with a sacrificial zeal and unsurpassed wit and wisdom. He was a good pen man with his letters and minutes of vestry meetings a joy to read.

After Vera Kerr resigned as Garvaghy Church organist I persuaded the teenager, Edna Ferguson, to take over. She remains in the post. Her choir in the years has earned the praise and gratitude of the little church and that of other churches, charities, and organisations for their work. I should add I had two sextons in Dromara, W.J. Moore and R.J. Rowan (Rabbie John) and one in Garvaghy, Jim Ferguson.

Robert Thompson was Rector's Churchwarden when I went to the parish and he remained in office until his sudden death in 1977. Robert was so highly esteemed that he was regarded as personifying what was to be expected in a deeply involved churchman. He made himself available for any chore and his value to St John's was inestimable. The same sentiments could be expressed about his successor Ernie Jess still in office when I retired from the parish. James Pollock, organist for nearly sixty years, who like Robert Thompson is memoralised in stained glass windows in St John's, was ever the enthusiastic musician and choir master. He served as church treasurer for many years and was the confidant and friend of clergy and people alike. Millar Kenny who succeeded as treasurer was a most efficient holder of an always difficult office.

There were several others who served St John's well in my time and ladies among them. It is a fact beyond dispute that the Church's indebtedness to its ladies can never be adequately expressed and Garvaghy church was equally well served.

They should represent that fellowship which is always cohesive and self sacrificing. If there is strength in numbers there can be an even greater strength where a people's deep commitment compensates for lack of numbers.

The Dromara glebe and its letting meant that I needed the help of glebe wardens who were practical farmers and constantly alive to the value of the land. I was fortunate in having the assistance and good advice of Robert Hart and then Howard Jess for Dromara and John Spiers for Garvaghy. We saw a remarkable increase in income from the land while all the time ensuring that it was maintained in good order. The glebe wardens were often the buffer between me and those renting the land though decisions were mine based on their good counselling. If I learned something about the working of the glebe land I became knowledgeable in its letting, use and maintenance.

21

NOTABLE EVENTS IN MY INCUMBENCY

There were so many important occasions in my incumbency of Dromara and Garvaghy in the churches and parish halls that to list them would mean going into such detail that the reader would be wearied. Suffice to say that every conceivable church event took place in our churches. I may be excused then for many omissions but there were happenings which deserve special mention. The services of dedication in St John's which included the Holy Table the gift of the Bell family on 3 July 1966, the Pollock window 17 November 1974, the rebuilt organ and the Thompson window 3 December 1978, and the Fee window 24 September 1982. The rededication of the organ requires explanation. For some time prior to 1978 the organ had been performing badly and it was agreed by the Select Vestry that something should be done about it. By chance I met Jim Moore, Rector of Broomhedge, in the Lagan Valley Hospital car park. With the organ very much in mind I asked him about organ builders not expecting any assistance in such a quest. He introduced me to Mr Charles Smethurst, Dunmurry, an Englishman, with long experience and great skill in the craft. We were to form a most valuable association with him and Mrs Smethurst who was his assistant. In an arrangement which meant that our men did the essential labouring work voluntarily the big task of rebuilding was accomplished at a great deal less of the cost if it had been done otherwise. An insistence of the organ builder was that it should be moved from its position in the chancel to the north transept. I had always hoped that this could be done, for placed in the chancel it took away from the whole north end of the church and hindered parishioners from getting a proper sight of the Sanctuary.

There were the 25th anniversary services to mark my silver jubilee in the parishes when the preacher was Gordon McMullan, Bishop of Clogher, understandably a great personal pleasure to us. In St John's Hall afterwards we were the recipients of some valuable gifts.

An unusual experience was to have a Sunday afternoon visit to St John's Church from the Dromore Historical Society (Roman Catholic) whose secretary was a neighbour, Fr. Bernard Treanor, on 8 May 1983. The lecture on the history of the church and parish was very well received by the large company of priests, nuns and lay members. This is perhaps the moment to say that Roman Catholic/Protestant relations were always very good in the area where good neighbourliness governed the words and actions of people.

In Garvaghy Church the dedication of oak pulpit, prayer desk and lectern in memory of Stanhope Squires, my predecessor, was a special event. So were the services to mark the 280th anniversary of the rebuilding of the church on 17 June 1979 when there was also a dedication of gifts. The churches had been developing a sense of Stewardship in the use of time, talent and money over the years. St John's had a most successful Stewardship Campaign which was introduced on 13 May 1984 and launched at a parish meal on 28 May. The campaign was organised by the Church of Ireland Stewardship Office and its director, Mr Erskine. We had the necessary ladies and gents committees and our parish controller was Philip McKinstry, who brought expertise and enthusiasm to his pivotal task.

Philip's interest in mission took him to Kenya to initiate a C.M.S. building and water project in July 1985. He was there again a year or two later with his family to benefit needy people with his practical Christianity. Winifred McKinstry was as deeply committed as her husband in good works. One of her many tasks was to edit the healing magazine. Like all busy people they were readily available for any task which had to be done.

22

THE ORANGE, THE CHURCH AND ME

When I joined the Loyal Orange Institution I had no thought of getting deeply involved in the organisation. I saw its value as a movement set for the defence of the Reformed Faith and with the capacity to draw together those of the Protestant denominations who have the same intention. As a unionist I saw it as a voice for people who had the same ambition to ensure that Northern Ireland remained part of the United Kingdom. And I regarded it as an opportunity to keep in touch with men in the community. The privileged place of the clerical chaplain in the Orange Order allows him the opportunity to emphasise Christian beliefs, and to advocate Christian ethical standards of behaviour, for the chaplain can be the teacher and the preacher of Orangeism.

The primary attraction for me in the Orange Order was its concentration on the Christian faith as preacher and practised in the early church and by the Protestant Reformers; its agreeableness with the theological emphases of the Church of Ireland, markedly biblical and liturgical in its ritual; given to friendship across the denominational divides; a brotherhood of shared beliefs and ethical principles.

I realised, human nature being as it is, that the plan and purpose of the organisation were idealistic, that the reality meant a constant striving to reach and to maintain the standards set by the founding fathers. Cognisant of the intention to encourage people to value and live by those models of belief and behaviour, that living is learning, thinking and doing. To have men trying to live by Christian faith and practice has to be a most laudable pursuit.

I found that the Order's intention was compatible with what my Church, and the Churches exist for, to worship God and to know Him in the person, worth and work of Jesus Christ.

The task of the Church is to persuade people to believe in God and to live their lives consonant with that faith and trust. The task of the Order is to encourage involvement of its members in the work and witness of the church in which they claim membership. Many Orangemen do that as office holders, and devout and devoted Churchmen.

It has had bishops and an archbishop, John Baptist Crozier, and many clergy of the Church of Ireland; Moderators of the General Assembly of the Presbyterian Church in Ireland and leaders from the other Protestant Churches.

The reasons for changes in attitudes of the churches to the Order in recent years are well known and their causes well documented and are in the public domain. The media here and everywhere, left no one in any doubt on the attitudes and actions of the many at every level interested in and affected by happenings and circumstances, often regrettable in their effect on life in Northern Ireland.

There has been, too, the growing secularism of a society in which churches and religiously orientated organisations have lost influence and effectiveness in their efforts to have the Christian voice heard necessarily, clearly and pungently.

True as an analysis of things generally there are successes with people and in places when there are positive responses to Christian work and witness.

The Somme Memorial Column, dedicated by me, and unveiled by Right Wor. Bro. James H. Molyneaux, MP, on Sunday 12th September 1993. (The Column was later moved inside the grounds of the Ulster Tower, close to the German Line)

The Orange Order remains a means of contact, church with men and they with it.

Whatever value is placed on church services with Orangemen in regalia in attendance they are opportunities for the church by its worship, singing, praying and preaching to encourage them to think on what it teaches of importance to them – Christian spiritual and ethical realities – and to hear the Word from God through people to people.

The controversies over the refusal of Churches to allow "Orange Services" are most regrettable. The reaction "You do not go where you are not welcome" has effects on Church and Order relationships not to be assessed by me that is for those who make decisions and live with them.

My own experience on the subject has been good. I have had no adverse situations to prevent me fulfilling engagements. I have nothing to add on the matter other than to say that judgements made need sensitive explanation and justification.

As a clerical chaplain, I used opportunities to contribute to the workings of the Order in an organisation where a hearing was guaranteed whatever the subject and the cut and thrust of debate was encouraged.

In Private, District, County, Grand Lodges and in my case the Imperial Council for World Orangeism, I had a voice and presence which was always determinedly centred on the faith to which the Institution is committed irrevocably.

I have persisted in membership at times when decisions taken by the Order were ill judged and controversial, and other clerical colleagues chose to disassociate themselves from it. I continue to believe in the values by which the Institution stands, while deeply regretting the inability or unwillingness of some members to keep the vows and promises made at their initiation. My experience has been that while the recruitment of brethren is a constant cause for concern, there is continuous need to question the applicants for membership on their perceptions of the Order, the honesty and sincerity it will expect from them and what it will require of them in character and conduct, in order to fulfil their obligations as good men and worthy citizens.

The Orange Institution, everywhere, has many admirable brethren who add considerably to the society and community to which they belong.

The fellowship of the lodge is so meaningful to them that it is demonstrated in the membership of aged brethren, Orangemen from their youth with their sons and grandsons in lodge with them.

23

FOND MEMORIES OF ORANGE

I have had very good experiences and happy relationships with brethren over the years. Regrettably many of them have passed on but I have pleasing remembrances of Orangemen of the calibre of Gordon Keyes, Les Saunders, W.S.K. Moffett (Canada); Bill Breadon, George McCullough, Al Bogan, James Gould, John Garland, Bill Best (USA); Walter Williams, Bill Crossley, Bishop Cyril Elliott, Sir George Clark, Sam Kinghan, Sam Magowan, Aiken McClelland, Ken Watson (Ireland). There are many others, of course, whose recall brings back shared, beneficial, joyous memories, and of incidents, events, and places which stay with me.

I have been privileged to travel for Orange Order engagements in Canada and America, Scotland and England, to retain contact with those jurisdictions, and with brethren in New Zealand and Australia whom I have known by attending with them the triennial sessions of the

Imperial Council. Personal reasons prevented me from accepting invitations from these countries.

The engagements were mostly as a preacher in this country, North and South, they make a large number over some fifty-five years. I have the happiest recollections of full churches, enthusiastic singing of well known hymns, reverence in worship and response to the readings and preaching in encouraging listening. It is not possible now for a preacher at Orange Services to preach in those great halls of other days the Grosvenor and the Wellington. I had that privilege and also in St Anne's Cathedral, the Assembly and Ulster Halls.

The largest ever Orange Order Twelfth demonstration was held on 29 September 1990 to mark the 300th anniversary of the Battle of the Boyne. It was a memorable Orange Order experience to conduct the service in the Strangford Playing Fields at Upper Malone and to lead in a ceremony of remembrance when after reciting the Laurence Binyon lines I asked for a silence during which there was no sound from that vast congregation.

As a speaker on Orangeism I gave lectures to the Theological Society of Trinity College Dublin (16.02.1970), at the University of Ulster (10.02.1970), at Queen's University to students in their centre, to the Irish School of Ecumenics in the crypt of St Anne's Cathedral; the Magee College, Londonderry, the Irish Council of Churches and European Churches seminar held in Edenmore Hotel, Whiteabbey.

These engagements as an Orangeman were augmented by study tours in Holland, based at De Haaf Bergen, and Haarlam, when my companions on the first one included the Rev Donald Gillies and Father

Padraig Murphy whose theological debates were to have the expected results – the one remained a totally convinced Presbyterian and the other an immovable Roman Catholic. The tours shared with churchmen, politicians, journalists, academics and industrialists. As I participated in them I was given the opportunity to get a most comprehensive view of government and local government in what I described in an essay-lecture as "The Tolerant Land." The main objective in the studies was to allow us to see how that country managed its affairs in another divided on religious and political beliefs and attitudes.

The trips were organised by Ralph Baxter, secretary of the Irish Council of Churches and a Dutch-Irish Committee who had the Rev At Van Rhijn and Father Andre Lescaris as the Dutch on the spot organisers and guides. The experiences were of value and significance to those who participated in them for we were shown something of government at the Hague – and various levels of administration in a country which appeared to be a model in how to have people live together in peace and with a good quality of life for all its citizens.

The effects of the studies were such that there were several post Holland meetings of attendees who studied ways and means by which Northern Ireland could benefit from the Dutch example. The differences there and here were such that they made it impossible to apply much of their methodology to our situation at that time, the Seventies, and the subject was pursued no further. It is worth adding, though that there were good things to be seen, strange to us then, that became acceptable to us thereafter.

Orange Order deputations were necessary to meet Prime Ministers and Secretaries of State prior to the prorogation of the Stormont

Parliament and after the imposition of Direct Rule by that most unfriendly Conservative Prime Minister, Edward Heath, because there were many questions to be put to them on about everything that mattered to people.

As a member of several of them then and with ominous signs of what was to happen in the future, they were memorable for their impressions of men in power wrestling with our problems tactically, reservedly and often non-commitedly on the answers they provided. We regularly left with added and different questions and doubts, however kindly we had been received, and we had that good reception however straight the talking across the table. The Prime Ministers we had sessions with were Terence O'Neill, James Chichester Clark and Brian Faulkner, Secretaries of State, William Whitelaw and Merlyn Rees. Each of them a personality who appeared to be fully committed to do his best for the province. Deputations, and there have been many of them since those days, have been reported on and questioned as to their value and usefulness.

Before writing an article 'The Parson in Politics' I wrote to William Whitelaw 16 April 1973 on the position of Church of Ireland clergy who might be invited to stand as candidates for the Northern Ireland Assembly. He replied to say that as the rules for Stormont applied, they would be ineligible. This meant that whatever the Church felt about clergy politicians the question was settled by the State. The other churches were free to act as they pleased, for there was no State restriction on their clergy. The Disestablishment of the Church of Ireland had not freed the clergy from a restriction as that for the Anglican Church in Wales had done. My question was about rights, for I knew of no Church of Ireland clergyman who wanted to enter politics professionally.

24

IRELAND'S UNREST IN THE TROUBLES

The beginnings of what were called the Troubles – an old description for civil unrest in Ireland – which lasted for thirty-eight years persuaded the Church of Ireland to set up an information centre at St Anne's Cathedral. The intention was to collate and disseminate news and views on the emerging crisis in Northern Ireland for the situation to be better understood by the church at large, and for it to speak on the subject learnedly when necessary. The thought of a centre was that of the Dean of Belfast, Cuthbert Peacocke, and the Archdeacon of Connor, John Mercer, and I as a writer was asked, to work in it as a helpful aid to a better understanding of what was happening.

Meetings on the venture were held on 30 August 1969 with Cuthbert Peacocke, John Mercer, George Quin, William Maourt, Gordon McMullan, Houston McKelvey and Ernest Long in attendance. At another on 1 September Mercer, McMullan, McKelvey and Long made arrangements for the launch of the Information Centre on 8 September. This was done with the media in attendance. It was manned on weekdays for the several months of its life by Gordon, Houston and me.

We were soon to realise that while the intention was a laudable one the use made of it did not warrant its continuance.

The growing unrest in the country and the difficulty there appeared to be in answering the charges made against the Unionist government, and Unionism in general, constrained me to write four folders in an attempt to explain the situation. There were published in 1972 by the Belfast County Grand Lodge as *A Series of Folders on Ulster Matters* and titled 'The Truth About Ulster', 'The Northern Ireland Problem', 'Ulster and the Way Ahead', 'The Role of the Orange Institution in Ulster'. There were several thousand copies for free distribution to the general public and they were so used in Scotland and England as well as Ireland. There was a reprinting in Australia when the name of the printer was added Gowans and Son PTY Ltd. 70-6406. A principal in the firm was John Gowans, Sydney, NSW, who served as Imperial Grand President of World Orangeism and Australian Grand Master. I became a columnist for The Orange Sentinel, Canada, in 1972 with a monthly feature 'The Ulster Scene'. It appeared for several years with Gordon Keyes as the editor and concluded with the revamp of the paper when Norman Richie took over.

In 1972 The Twelfth Magazine was founded on my initiative, and Martin Smyth and I were the co-editors. An annual, it has been published every year since with the dual task of enlightening the members, and people at large, on the thinking of Orangemen on many subjects; and by its sales adding considerably to the Order's charitable gifts to worthy causes.

The monthly newspaper of the Order in Ireland was launched in January 1973 again on my initiative but with the benefit of the highly skilled professionalism of Douglas Sloan. We worked together on the paper for many years, encouraged by the officers and member of Grand Lodge and especially by Grand Secretary, Walter Williams. The growth of the paper and the necessity of a more commercialised approach to it brought with it a Board of Management with Billy Kennedy as its convenor. This allowed Douglas and I to withdraw from the joint editorship and for Billy Kennedy, a most knowledgeable and well accredited journalist to take over. He and Brian Courteny, who assisted him, were protégés of Douglas Sloan when he was editor of the Portadown News. We use the old cliché that the paper goes from strength to strength, and since Billy Kennedy's tenure as editor, under Dr David Hume.

I continue to write 'Comment' for the paper and on the request of Billy Kennedy added a devotional essay now called 'The Pulpit'. A number of these were published in November 2006 titled *Think on These Things*, the first purely religious book to be published by the Grand Lodge of Ireland and by its Schomberg Press.

My writing for Orange publications has meant monthly contributions 'The Ulster Forum' in The Orange Torch, Scotland, and occasionally in the New Zealand and Australian quarterlies. It was in 1974 that I was asked to draft the Twelfth Resolutions on Faith and State. I did thus until 2006 and 2007 when the draft of the State Resolution was by the Grand Orange Lodge Ireland Office.

The intention behind whatever I have written on Orangeism and Unionism is to be fair and balanced in my treatment of matters of consequence to me, and expectantly to people generally. I repeat what I have said elsewhere, I write to enlighten, educate and entertain. And always there is the desire to treat people with respect, however they may differ from me in their attitudes to so many things. It is always incumbent on a writer to speak of what he believes and how he feels on subjects that are important to him and to listen to what others say and believe about the same matters. It is a good philosophy – something to say, say it; nothing to say, say nothing.

25

MY WORK IN WRITING

I wrote a number of pamphlets, from 1963 and to 1983. They dealt with social problems and were published by Church of Ireland Temperance and Social Welfare Society, the Temperance Committee of the Diocese of Connor, Down and Dromore, the Church of Ireland Board of Social Responsibility, the Methodist Council on Social Welfare, and the Down and Dromore and Connor Home Mission Committee.

They had titles *Careful as You Go* (1963), *Say Why, Say When?* (1964), *Bet You Shouldn't* (1965), *Life is not for Kicks* (1968), *Say No to Drugs* (1970), *On the Run from Reality* (1971), *Violence and Morality* (1972), *Hold Your Tongue* (1973), *What about Justice – Truth, Charity, Conscience?* (1974), *Freedom and Responsibility* (1975), *Ireland in the Larger Community* (1976), *The Family* (1976), and *Personal Evangelism, the One with the Other* (1983).

This writer's intention was to say something simply and usefully on topics in discussion or debate, for the matters considered in them were causes of concern to people personally and collectively.

It was person to person communication, conversation, with a careful, thoughtful, sensitive and economical use of words and thoughts aimed at changing attitudes to what remains of crucial importance to us as a people among them alcohol, drugs, gambling and their effects on those who use and misuse them. Other matters of the moment were dealt with and everything viewed from a Christian perspective on life in a society increasingly secularist and materialistic, unaffected by the norms of the religiously orientated ideas and attitudes of other days.

The use of folders/pamphlets, a teaching and telling method of regular usage and for many purposes had the advantage of being easy to read on receipt or to pocket for a more thoughtful perusal of their contents. That they were distributed freely and in large numbers meant that many had the opportunity to read them, and to be influenced or unaffected by them. I echoed St Paul when he said "I believed and therefore did I speak" (2 Corinthians 4:13).

The Grand Lodge of Ireland publications, *A Celebration 1690-1990: The Orange Institution*; and *Steadfast in Faith and Freedom – 200 years of Orangeism 1795 - 1995* are compendiums of the history, philosophy and policy of the organisation. Lavishly illustrated they give a panoramic view of the Institution worldwide. They do much more when by profiles of kings and great men, and the recounting of events meaningful to the movement, they teach lessons on a past which for many remains a reason for remembrance and celebration.

They had Billy Kennedy as editor, and contributors whose work was well presented and painstakingly researched in a format attractively produced, well illustrated and easy to read.

My contributions in *A Celebration* were 'The Orange Institution – the Early Years', 'The Seige of Londonderry', 'Two Kings in Combat at Boyne Water', 'The Orange Family Worldwide' and 'United States of America'; and in *Steadfast* 'International Orangeism', 'Origins and Beginnings' and 'The Imperial Orange Council'.

I add the comment the Grand Lodge should ensure by constant reference to these books, that this literacy heritage is valued and that frequent use is made of it. And the reminder – any thinking on the future of the Orange Institution must recognise that this is not an organisation age. Male fraternal societies are affected in a situation where men are no longer separatist as they were in other days with them going their way and wives theirs.

While it was never my intention to be more than a lodge chaplain, I found myself in high office and there could have been higher offices if I had consented to stand for them. Only once did I allow myself to be pressed to contest an election in the Institution. It turned out to be something of a fiasco, for those who approached me about the office of County Grand Master of Belfast assured me that the then Grand Master, John Bryans, at eighty-four years of age would not be standing again. It turned out to be a presumption on their part for he had determined to go on. I was unaware of this different situation and when the election took place on 9 November 1965 and John Bryans was also nominated, he won by one vote, twenty-eight to twenty-seven. I was surprised by the figures, for the holder of an office can be expected to receive a number of sympathy votes. I discovered afterwards that Bryans had sought and been promised support from members who had not known of the approach to me. Ironically one of those who pressed me to stand was absent from the election meeting. His reason for non-attendance was regarded as a feeble excuse. I was relieved at the result for had I known what was to happen I would not have been in the contest. I was the first to congratulate John Bryans for whom I had admiration and respect. I took the result to be an escape for I had no wish to hold an executive office with its heavy demands on my time. Had I been elected my tenure of office would have been short, for that was the agreement I had with my sponsors. When at another time I was asked to allow myself to be nominated for an even higher office I refused and repeated that decision on an asking after another interval.

When John Bryans retired as Grand Master a meeting of senior officers was held at Brownlow House, Lurgan, to select a successor. When I was nominated to fill the vacancy I refused. I gave three reasons for that decision – "I couldn't give the time and attention required in such a busy office; I couldn't afford the expense; and the family wouldn't want to see even less of me."

While I received assurances that the first two of my difficulties could be eased somewhat, the third had to be a matter for me. I was not to be persuaded to change my mind and the Rev. W. Martin Smyth was appointed. He held the office for twenty-four years. My warm and well earned tribute to him, on his resignation from office, was published in The Orange Standard.

I was happy to be elected a Grand Chaplain of the Grand Lodge of Ireland and Imperial Chaplain of the Orange Council of the World because these offices were in keeping with my sense of pastoral responsibility and opportunity.

The duty and commitment of Orange Order chaplains was clear to me when issues of concern to them and the Institution surfaced. It may be that because of my literary work in Orangeism I became involved in meetings of chaplains where consideration was given to pressing problems with the intention of influencing decisions. I recall a meeting of Church of Ireland chaplains in the CIYMS hall on 28 June 1966 which coincided with one for Presbyterian Chaplains in the Assembly Hall. Later in the day I went to met with J.C. Parke and Eric Boreland to compare notes on the meetings. Church of Ireland chaplains from Clogher diocese met with me and Michael Dewar at Dromara Rectory in 1969. There was a Church of Ireland chaplain's meeting at Christ Church Hall, Lisburn, on 6 November 1970 when I read an essay 'Orange Reality'. There was another meeting in St John's Hall, Dromara, on 11 October 1971 and again in The House of Orange on 7 September 1975 when I read a paper 'The Orange Order and the Churches'. There was a conference for chaplains in Brownlow House, Lurgan, 20 November 1989 when papers were read by Roy Vallely and Robert Dickinson and I had one 'Religion in Ireland in the 17th century'.

I took part in the arrangements which the Ulster Unionist Party and the Orange Institution made for the jubilee of the signing of the Ulster Covenant in 1912. The highlights of the celebrations included a Covenant brochure; a banquet in the City Hall, Belfast, when I proposed the toast of the City of Belfast on 28 September 1962; and a mammoth demonstration at the Show Grounds, Balmoral on the 29th. My article 'The Birth of Ulster' with illustrations made up the front page of the Newsletter on that date. My pamphlet *The Covenant* was published on

12 November 1962. Centenary celebrations of the Belfast County Grand Lodge were held in 1963 and they included an Ulster Hall dinner on 8 November. Invited to write a short history of the Lodge it was published on 2 July 1963.

The flags which carried at the head of the Belfast Twelfth procession for some years were dedicated in the Clifton Street Hall in memory of the well known and most efficient secretary of the Belfast County and Grand Lodges, Harry Burdge, J.P., at which I gave the eulogy. Burdges' assistant, Walter Williams succeeded him as Grand Secretary on 11 December 1963 to begin a twenty-five year record of exemplary services to Orangeism here, and abroad as Imperial Secretary.

One of the big events in Irish Orangeism was the specialist Lodge of Research. LOL 1994, which received recognition from Grand Lodge at its inception, was the "brainchild" of Aiken McClelland, a highly esteemed local historian and specialist in Orange Order and Freemasonry studies. It was his involvement with the Masonic Lodge of Research, which give him the idea of a similar lodge for the Orange Institution. He made contact with Ernest Long, Orange chaplain and Rector of Dromara and Garvaghy. Together the Primary School principal and popular clergyman while recognising the similarities, but more the dissimilarities of the two organisations and the indebtedness the one to the other in 1795 in its structures, concluded that with very different terms of reference there was merit in the suggestion.

They quickly sought support, if a lodge was to be launched, and it came from Bob Jones, Technical school vice-principal, Ballynahinch, primary school principal colleague of Aiken McClelland, Robert Wright, and Sam Magowan MP. With the encouragement of Walter Williams,

Grand Secretary, the lodge was instituted with due ceremony. These lodge origins, and continuing activities, are archival material in the possession of the lodge.

I must add the essential observation that Orangeism and Freemasonry are often mistakenly joined as kin-type organisations. Their aims and objectives, in essence, are very different. Where Freemasonry has a relatively little religious content to its ceremonies the Orange Order is, by its ritual, a Christian organisation and deliberately committed to that faith, and the duties and responsibilities consonant with it.

So that from the outset the Orange Lodge of Research had a clear objective to study, collate, and publish material on the subjects inherent to its thinking on Orangeism, Unionism and Protestantism. That was exemplified in the many studies presented to the lodge in papers which were often published for a general readership thereafter.

The Lodge has four meetings a year and visits have been paid to places of special interest in Williamite, Irish and Orange history. The first on 12 September 1964 was to the site of the Battle of the Diamond, Dan Winter's Cottage and the Orange Museum at Loughgall where Orangeism began. There were visits to Dublin 7 May 1965 to see the Williamite china and glass in the National Museum, the tapestries in the Bank of Ireland and the Lord Mayoral Chain which was the gift of William III to the city; to Londonderry, 7 June 1966 and the cathedral with its artefacts of the Seige and to the Boyne on whose banks the battle was fought, on 3 May 1969. Each visit had expert lecturers to guide us through what we saw and heard.

An enthusiastic member of the Lodge, Dr. Richard Hayward, author, actor, film maker and ballad singer, was killed in a car accident on 13 October 1964. The first lodge memorial service was held in Sandy Row Orange Hall on 7 November 1964 when I paid the tribute to him. That duty has fallen on me several times since.

When it was decided by the Grand Lodge Press Committee to publish *A New Historical Appreciation* of the Institution on 13 September 1965 three members were asked to tackle the task: Michael Dewar had the Williamite period, John Brown, the origins of the Institution and Ernest Long Orangeism and Unionism since 1886. The book was published in 1967 and there have been several reprintings and a continuing use of it.

Since then there have been a number of publications, though none specifically about Orangeism. There was *William of Orange*, published for the tercentenary Imperial Council at Brixham, Devon, in September 1988 with authors Michael Dewar (England), David Bryce (Scotland) and Ernest Long (Ireland). The book published to mark the tercentenary of the Battle of the Boyne in May 1990 is a well produced and illustrated book for which Michael Dewar and I were major contributors.

I had constantly advocated the value and usefulness of the written word and regretted that Orangemen had been reluctant to express their views by the permanence of print. However when I suggested an annual Belfast County Lodge magazine the idea was readily accepted. And so *The Twelfth* appeared on 30 June 1966 with Martin Smyth sharing editorial responsibility with me. The booklet has appeared every year since and from the beginning the profits from its sales have gone to local charities. In 1972 when Grand Lodge accepted the need for a monthly newspaper cum magazine to be co-edited by W.P. Sloan and

S.E. Long the first issue of The Orange Standard was launched at a press conference in the Europa Hotel, Belfast, on 19 January 1973. The paper continues publication while many other Protestant and Unionist papers have come and gone.

It has tried to be both a journal and a newspaper. It has never been easy to strike the necessary balance nonetheless. It has been a medium of information and education of value to Orangemen and a source to be tapped by all who are interested in the cultural, political and religious attitudes of the organisation.

'The Orange Standard Award' presented by Grand Master Robert Saulters for 'lifelong achievement', at Coleraine Town Hall, 31 January 2009

The editorial policy of the paper has been displayed in its thoughtful and sensitive approach to matters of concern to the Institution and the community it serves. It has avoided the sensational, and merely provocative, persisting in treating its subjects rationally and with controlled emotion. There has been no avoiding the problems numerous in a society constantly under attack from terrorists and regularly from media people and politicians whose understanding of the situation can be deficient. The Orange Institution has had to face the denunciations of people who have never made an effort to understand what Orangeism is about and why it has retained the support of many thousands of men in a loyalty which is likely to be for the whole of their lives.

I produced other booklets *Rather Be An Ulsterman* published 7 July 1972 and *The Orange Institution* 28 September 1978. *Carson* appeared on 25 June 1968 with its third printing re-titled *Man for Ulster* and with a cover carrying a portrait of Sir Edward Carson it appeared 23 December 1969.

At the Orange Community Awards held in Coleraine Town Hall on 31 January 2009, I was formally recognised for my contribution to the Orange Institution and wider community, and presented with 'The Orange Standard Award' for lifelong achievement.

26

COMING TO AMERICA

I have been fortunate to have many worthwhile experiences through my association with the Orange Order. Bill Crossley and I were invited to go to Canada and America to explain the Ulster crisis from a viewpoint very different to that being heard from Irish republicans and their sympathisers and supporters in North America. We left for Canada on 16 June 1969 and were the speakers at an Ulster Convention in the Skyline Hotel, Ottawa, where the Grand Lodge of Canada had its sessions. The event in a full banqueting hall was a good start to the tour. We were privileged to visit the Houses of Parliament and to have a lengthy conversation with John Diefenbaker, former Prime Minister and Leader of the Opposition, after hearing him attacking the policies of the Prime Minister, Pierre Trudeau. In Toronto on Sunday 22 June I was the evening preacher in St Paul's Church, Bloor Street, sometimes compared in size, style and furnishings to Salisbury Cathedral. Bill and I were the speakers at the second Ulster rally in the

King Edward Hotel on the 23rd. We were deeply indebted to Gordon Keyes, Canadian Grand Secretary, for the arrangements he made for our welfare, and engagements, and to him and Mrs Keyes for much enjoyed hospitality and for showing us some of the sights of Toronto.

We arrived in Boston on 24 June to stay in the Somerset Hotel. The Brookline lodge and its officers Bill Breadon and George McCracken were the men behind our invitation. We had a rally at Brookline and took part in television and radio programmes. The television experience was happy enough with an attractive interviewer Mrs Van Camp who was well known as a stage and screen actress. We had had to explain much about Ulster to the station manager, Mr Cavfield, who admitted to ignorance of the subject while contending that his company had left it alone.

The radio programme was different. We made half of a foursome to debate the Ulster Problem. Our "opponents" were a Protestant Episcopal clergyman, just returned from a two-weeks visit to Belfast and a Harvard professor, a thorough going republican. The two hour debate began at 11pm with a moderator anxious to be impartial. The debate was not troublesome to us, the problem came with the phone-in, something little known on British radio at the time. Because the lines were hogged by republicans the questions were predictable. The moderator occasionally defended us when he thought we were being attacked unreasonably and in intemperate language. We had one pleasing interlude when a lady rang in, not with a question but to say she had waited long to hear English spoken properly on that station and it had happened as she listened to two Ulstermen.

After our two hour stint we enjoyed the hospitality of the station for we got a plastic cup of cold water each after asking for it. Our hosts appeared to be satisfied with our performances and one of them made a recording of the radio programme. The large tape was sent to me but as I have distaste for "inquests" I have never listened to it. Incidentally the audience figure was said to be a possible two million.

I had the pleasure of preaching at St Paul's Church, Brookline, on 20 June and especially because former Dromara residents, Jim Smith and William and Alex Mercer were in the congregation with their families. Brothers and sisters of these men were my parishioners in Dromara.

Again Bill Crossley and I were greatly benefited by the kindness of our hosts at Brookline, Bill and Sue Breadon, Susan Corbett and George McCracken. We got briefcases from Bill and George and I have used mine ever since.

After Boston we travelled by bus to New London and by ferry to Long Island and Cutchogue where we had a short holiday with Al and Mary Bogan.

When Bill Crossley left for home on 1 July I stayed to speak at a meeting in Norway Hall, Glen Head, Long Island, on 2 July. The Bogans took me on 3 July to Philadelphia. As the guest of Lewis and Diane McCorkell – he was then Supreme Grand Master of the USA – I saw something of the 4 July Independence Day celebrations. The McCorkells were members of the local band and took part in a colourful parade with a picnic as part of it. The Philadelphia rally on 5 July was also well attended and memorable because the heat and humidity drenched me with sweat. It was worse than at Boston where Crossley and I had to go into the air-conditioned stores to get out of the heat of the street.

Lewis McCorkell showed me a few of the sights of Philadelphia, Independence Hall, Betsy Ross' House, Christ Church were George Washington and the founding fathers of the USA worshipped and where the ECUSA was founded. He showed me the battlefield at Valley Forge and the Museum there. I flew out from Philadelphia for home via New York on 6 July after an unforgettable experience of Canada and America and of the kindness of many people.

I was in America again in 1971 with Martin Smyth to be speakers at the Orange Order sponsored Labour Day Rally in the grounds of the Orange Home at Hatborough, Pennsylvania, on 6 September. The home was the crown of American Orangeism, a proud achievement of charitable minded and activated men and women, for the ladies association has been much engaged in the scheme. Originally used for orphans the home was to house senior citizens for several years. The visit was arranged by Bill Best, ex-Belfast man and New York travel agent. I had a frightening experience when after a few days with the Bests in New York I left to be the guest of Basil and Mrs Doloughan at New Castle, Delaware. I left by bus late at night with an arrangement to be met at Wilmington bus station for the short journey to New Castle. In the bus station Bill discovered that I would have a lengthy stop over at Philadelphia. He promised to ring Basil asking him to meet me in the Philadelphia bus terminus. When I got to Philadelphia I found there was a bus leaving shortly for Wilmington. Not sure that Bill had got through to Basil I boarded the bus. It transpired that he had made contact and settling in the bus I was being paged out of earshot through the station speakers. When I reached Wilmington I found the bus depot closed up and in darkness. It was now after midnight and the only people around and at a distance appeared to be the worse for drink. I felt lost. Just then a man appeared and acting on the old adage, "When you're lost ask a policeman", I enquired about the nearest police station. I was shattered when he said that he had no idea, for he was making a first visit to America from Hamilton, Ontario and had been on the bus with me. A poorly lighted building across the way encouraged us to seek advice there. It turned out to be a small railway station without people but with two telephones. I had the Wilmington number of Walter Wilson, Grand Secretary of the Orange Order in the USA. I rang him and when he heard where I was he told me "That's no place to be. Stay where you are and I'll come for you." The Canadian, who had borrowed an American coin from me got through to his friends who collected him as Walter arrived for me.

Walter stayed until Basil caught up with us and while we waited I pointed to a neon-signed hotel in near where we were, "I thought I would have spent the night there." He replied, "You might have regretted that for it has a couple of murders a month." He may have been joking but I was willing to believe it as I looked at the sleasy area around. He told me I had left the bus at the wrong stop, for the depot was on the other side of the city. I asked Walter what one could do in a similar situation. He said contact should be made with the Travellers' Aid Society or the Salvation Army. In a review of a book on the Salvation Army I mentioned the advice to receive a letter from the Information Office thanking me for the reference to a facility of theirs which needed to be better known.

When Bill Best was installed as Supreme Grand Master of the USA on 13 August 1972 the impressive ceremony was in the Biltmore Hotel,

New York and Martin Smyth and I were present. Before the installation I planned to visit my Dromara colleague, Renwick, and Mrs Wright, who had gone to the Reformed Presbyterian Church at Beaver Falls, near Pittsburg, on 27 April 1969. At the bus station toothache, which had been playing me up for the few days I had stayed with Bill and Mamie Best at Forest Hills, made me so miserable that they persuaded me to stay another two nights with them and then to fly to Pittsburg. The Wrights met me at the Pittsburg airport and took me to the manse where I spent a few very happy and enlightening days. But before there could be any joy something had to be done about my now much swollen face. Renwick took me to his dentist, who while unable to extract the offending molar managed to ease it, and supplied me with some medication. The time and care he took with me was a worry, for I had heard of the very high cost of dental care in America. I wondered how I could pay his bill but when I asked him for it he said, "There is no charge, because first you are a visitor to our country, and secondly because you are a minister you will not have any money." The Wrights took me to Geneva College at Beaver Falls, a Reformed Church foundation and to the Theological Seminary of the Church of Pittsburg, and there was a trip on the river. After the Beaver Falls visit I flew to Philadelphia and a house meeting on Ulster at the home of James and Irene Howie formerly Ballymena and Donegal respectively. James Howie and I went to a market where Amish folk were selling their greengrociers to learn something of these remarkably devout and highly disciplined people who disdain modern dress and conveniences. I went by car from Philadelphia to Wilmington and the friends there to stay with Walter and Sallie Wilson. It was on this trip that I was first shown Longwood Gardens, Penn. My guides were Ann Hamilton and Norman McCullough both ex-Belfast. Norman was most generous even noting my selection of picture slides so that when I got to the pay desk my account had been settled. He entertained me to a meal and afterwards showed me to the Wilmington Masonic Temple.

We left Wilmington as a party for the convention. It was a return for me to New York where I had been from 29 July until I went to Beaver Falls. I was shown around New York by Bill Best and Bob Watson, ex-Belfast, and it was Bob who took me to the cathedral of St John the Divine. I was duly impressed by the size and magnificence of the building and by the fact that further construction had been halted because the church authorities had decided that it would be wrong to build when so many in the city were in poverty with hunger and homelessness all around. Sited near Harlem we had a look at some of that deprivation beside the cathedral in the tenement blocks.

In a break from the Convention, Charles Reynolds, ex Shankill Road, and clerical general secretary of a missionary organisation with his office in the Inter-Church Centre on Riverside Drive, took us to meet Father Donald R. Campion, editor, and staff members of the prestigious Roman Catholic monthly *The American*. When I wrote about American church publications this one was rated highly. After the Convention at which we had been given opportunities to address the men's and women's grand lodges, for as in Canada they meet simultaneously at the conventions, I went by bus with the other delegates from Connecticut and Massachusetts to Boston and a few days with the Brendons who hosted a party for me to meet the friends of 1969. My travelling case was mislaid on the Boston to New York flight but after a delay it turned up. Martin and I were seen off for home by Bill and Mamie, Bill's brother George and Jim Smith who worked in Best Way Travel with the brothers.

I was in Canada again in 1974 for the Canadian Black Institution celebrations at Niagara Falls. I had seen the magnificent Falls in 1969 but this time a group of us were taken beneath them, oil skins and all, on the invitation of Jim Molyneaux. After the Orange and Black convention I had a speaking engagement in Rochester, New York State. I was taken there by car, for my host John Garland, an enthusiastic champion of the Ulster cause, was a visitor at the Niagara sessions. I had another example of coincidence when out for a morning stroll I looked in at a Lutheran Church. There I met the pastor who told me he had ministered to the Lutheran congregation in University Road, Belfast, near to All Saint's Church, whose rector, Sidney Smart, had been a close friend. I had finished a series of evening services at All Saints Church only a few weeks before. John Garland and I visited the Rochester Anglican Cathedral and met the dean who told me of an ordination service for the next Sunday and invited me to take part in it. I had to refuse what would have been an interesting experience for I was to preach at St Stephen's – on – the Mount Church, Hamilton, Ontario, that day. The rector of St Stephen's was Desmond Fleming who had served in our diocese as rector of Ardglass. He showed me something of church life in his city and diocese and how well the clergy were looked after educationally and recreationally.

I stayed in Hamilton with John and May Monroe. He and I attended the funeral of a friend in Orillia, the sunshine city of Stephen Leacock, and there he visited an old college friend of Shaftesbury House days, Eric Beggs and Ruth, his wife, both of whom I had known from Roden Street days. He was Presbyterian minister there and enjoying a good ministry in a most responsive congregation with a fine church plant and one of the best organs in Canada. In Orillia I had another glimpse of the North Amercian way of death, the elaborate preparations of the corpse for burial or cremation, the large and expensive caskets and the beautiful funeral parlours. It was strange to receive advertising pens and cards from very efficient funeral directors. The experience was the subject of an article I wrote copies of which were requested by undertakers here.

The Imperial Orange Council of World Orangeism had its 1982 triennial sessions in Toronto. On this visit I preached at St Peter's Church, Windsor, whose rector was William Carson, a friend of Gordon Keyes. The Carsons collected me in Toronto at the Orange Twelfth demonstration there and took me the long distance to Windsor. The service in a new church was most impressive and I found William Carson to be a well of information on the Anglican Church of Canada. When the Carsons took me to their cabin on the lake I was disappointed to be unable to stay for the invited few days for I had to return for the opening of the Council in Toronto. My driver was a young lady friend of the Carsons and a most skilful motorist.

After the triennial which had the customary outings in which we visited Kingston and Deseronto, where we were entertained by the Indian Orangemen to a programme of songs and dances, Ken Watson and I accepted invitations to visit New York, Wilmington and Boston. Travelling by Peoples' Express aircraft from Buffalo, where we were taken by John Garland on his way to Rochester, to Newark, New Jersey. By bus to New York we found ourselves in Times Square station late at night. As we were going to the home of Bob Hetherington at North Bronx we had to ask a policeman to confirm the way we should travel. When I sought information from one of them he looked at my clerical collar and said, "Father, you must get away from this as quickly as possible for this place can be very dangerous for strangers. Look at how many of us are on duty here." He recognised my brogue and told me his father was a Sligo man. He also told me what platform to go to and wished me well. On the platform a railway man told us the train number, and added that the journey would take thirty-five minutes. We wondered why he timed it for us. We saw the reason from the train for all the station names had been blotted out with graffiti. It took us thirty-five minutes until we saw Bob Hetherington on the platform waiting for us.

When we travelled into New York next day it was by express bus which had no stops after we boarded it, for to stop in the area we travelled through would have been dangerous. On the Sunday morning we attended service at Krogg's Neck Presbyterian Church where the woman minister was a good preacher though there were those in the congregation who spoke of "having only a woman minister".

Wilmington was a pleasant break for me with the Wilsons. Ken went on to stay with friends in Washington. We met up on the Saturday at Wilmington bus depot and were on our way by coach to Newark, NJ. where we got a People's Express plane for Boston. There we were the guests of James and Ellen Gould, the most alert and active elderly people I have ever met and that in spite of James' strokes and Ellen's surgery. They recruited their friend Frank Foster to be our guide. Frank a prominent Anglican layman increased my knowledge of the ECUSA and together with the Goulds showed us much of the area around when we toured and saw towns like Gloucester and Salem and the battlefields at Lexington and Concord. We enjoyed going around Boston city centre on our own and spending time in the famous buildings and churches there. From my first visit across the Atlantic I had gathered written and pictorial material on the churches I visited. My church based articles appeared in The Church of Ireland Gazette. The more general interest ones appeared in The Mourne Observer and The Orange Standard. The many transparies I gathered helped me to give talks on the trips.

We attended a Sunday morning communion service at Holy Trinity Boston, the church of the famous preacher, author and bishop Philips Brooks. He was so much involved in the community that Boston has many evidences of his influence. The author of the hymn O *Little Town of Bethlehem* died after a brief episcopate as Bishop of Massachusetts. We were impressed by the very large attendance at the service. The celebrant was assisted at the administration of the sacrament by five priests, the staff of four and two retired clergymen, one of them Don Dewert had been the rector of Brookline when I preached there in 1969. He recognised me and reminded me of the visit.

The Goulds hosted a garden party at which I resumed friendships made in 1969 and 1972. It was especially pleasing to see again Sue Breadon, Bill's widow. By then George McCracken and Susan Corbett had also passed away.

Ellie and I were in the USA August 1986 the guests of the Supreme Grand Lodge at their sessions. Afterwards we spent a week with the Wilsons. We visited Longwood Gardens and the Orange Home at Hatborough and holiday places on the coast towards Maryland. At the sessions it was a particular pleasure to see Sallie Wilson installed as Supreme Grand Mistress of the Ladies Association of the USA. My interest in American Orangeism made it easy for me to answer the request to write about it. My *Short History of the Orange Institution in the USA* was published in America and by the Lodge of Research.

27

LET'S GO DUTCH

My connections with Orangeism and Unionism had me invited to go with other religious and community representative people to the Netherlands on 28 September to 3 October 1973. A Dutch committee with government aid was trying to help in the Ulster crisis by having us, Protestants and Roman Catholics, consider the accommodation to differences in a Dutch setting. The Dutch leaders in the project were the Rev. A.E. Van Rhyn, a Lutheran pastor and Father Andre Lasaris, a Roman Catholic priest. The Irish organiser was the Rev. Ralph Baxter, the Irish Council of Churches. We met at the de Haaf Centre near Bergen-on-Sea a well sited and comfortable modern building. The discussions were useful but expectantly inconclusive. One advantage was to be encouraged to study in depth the attitudes of political parties, the police and people in Northern Ireland and to see our state over and against that of another society divided on confessional lines, which I was to describe as 'The Tolerant Land'. We recognised the imperative that while in Holland division was on denominational lines there was common loyalty to country. That fundamental difference made the comparison between it and N.I. We were shown places of interest and met people whose devotion to their country was absolute. The quiet, sensitive, rational, philosophy for living by the Dutch was a revelation to us. We could admire what we could not emulate.

It happened when Donald Gillies and I attended a nearby Lutheran Church. We had not a word of the language, but as it was a baptismal service we could make sense of what was happening. Just as the minister began his sermon a lady slipped us a peppermint each. I sucked mine to find that it had dissolved as the sermon ended. Because Donald had the same experience we concluded that this was the Dutch way to time the sermon. I was reminded of the preacher who used a wee sweetie to time his sermons until someone substituted a like white button and he went on and on.

Because we looked for tangible results from the visit to the Netherlands there were follow up meetings for those who had participated in it. They were held at Queen's in 1974. In hindsight it should have been obvious that after the first one when everyone attended and no sign was given that anything of consequence would emerge to encourage change in the Ulster situation the others would be little more than "wind past the ears." Having said that it should be added that some of us made friends and were benefited by unexpected friendships.

I was with another group to the Netherlands in March 1975, politicians of SDLP, Alliance, UPNI and NIPL with seven media men. Again de Haaf was the meeting place. The discussions were useful if only for the clarification of our differences in aims and aspirations. There were studies again of Dutch political attitudes and responses.

Among the engagements was a visit to the Hague to see the parliament at work and to be advised of the difference between the Dutch and British government and parliamentarians. We were shown a little of the intensive horticulture and agriculture industries of the Westland's and at police headquarters in Amsterdam a most fluent English speaking head of the CID made us aware of methods of policing in his city. When we asked about policemen on the beat he explained that his force was against "police in tins." There was a visit to den Helder and a meeting with the Minister for Housing with his emphasis on the refurbishment of older properties. The new housing there, and especially that for senior citizens, was most impressive. The Institute of Cultural Relations gave us insight into how the religiously divided country managed to order and maintain itself. There was one follow up meeting at Queen's on 13 April 1975. The reality was that on this visit while party leaders faced each other with their differences, and were questioned by media people, there was no movement among them. The learning and sharing process is such that there must have been some benefit to the participants. Incidentally a few of them abandoned politics.

The third Netherlands visit was on 16 to 20 February 1979 to the Oud Poelgeest centre in the old palace near Haarlem. The party included Ulster Unionist Party politicians and party officers with Harry West the UUP leader and a few of us who made up the staff for the occasion. They were shown much of what the others had seen with a larger concentration on Netherlands politics. The visit to the Hague and a hearing of the House in session was followed by explanations of political structures from three party leaders in a council chamber. The Unionists were enlightened on the Dutch pillar system – Roman Catholic, Protestant and Socialist – not from political analysts but from men who had to make it work in coalition government, the normal of Holland. The Unionists were quick to point out that the Dutch philosophy of separateness and sharing in power was possible because there was a shared loyalty to their country whereas in Northern Ireland there was divided loyalty.

The visit to Westland included attendance at a Dutch auction, often heard of but never before seen by many of us. The buyers from their raised gallery with telephones at their hands to keep contact with their employers, found it all perfectly easy. The old city of Delfth was a reminder of an age long gone and to have a meal in the cellar of the palace of William the Silent was to think of William of Orange. In that city we were informed of Dutch marriage regulations which required a religious ceremony followed by a civil one.

Again there was a visit to den Helder, a study of housing, and a look at its fishing and fish factories. Some of the group could copy the Dutch and swallow slivers of raw fish. I was not one of them.

As to housing we like to think that the groups who visited the Netherlands influenced housing development in Northern Ireland. James O'Hara who was a member of the first one became chairman of the Northern Ireland Housing Executive.

There was a UUP/Dutch reception in the Stormont Hotel, Belfast, when Iris Bakker, At Van Ryln and Andre Lasaris were the guests. The Dutch/Northern Ireland Committee had a meeting at Queen's University

Belfast on 2 May 1979 when the guest speaker was Professor Tiensen and contact with it ceased. It appeared that the patience of the Dutch in their effort to help us had been exhausted.

While the Dutch visits had no tangible results in political change we met people, of whom we had heard in uncomplimentary terms to find that we could be friends with them. I found a friend in J.H. Campbell of the Cameron Commission, well known as an educationalist who encouraged me to do some advanced studies in Orangeism and Unionism and though I made some progress in his time the intention reached fruition only in my retirement.

28

RENEWAL IN THE ORANGE

I have constantly, and consistently, paid compliment to Orangemen for their life-long commitment, and self-sacrificing zeal, for the causes inherent in the organisation – Fraternalism, Unionism and Protestantism.

While the fellowship of the Brotherhood is to be valued everywhere for its shared value and experiences, and its determination here to maintain the Union of Great Britain and Northern Ireland, it is the emphasis on the Christian faith in the Reformed Tradition that has mattered most to me.

My especial concentration in the Institution has been on what to me is fundamental and primary, devotion to Jesus Christ as Lord and Saviour. The capacity to make people mindful of what is of utmost importance to us, and should be to them – the Christian faith and the way of life consonant with it, means that it is our duty to ensure that our witness to it is strengthened by our outreach to others and in convincing them of its continuing relevance. We may do this in several ways but I value the written word as the most effective, for it has a permanence, in whatever form, not available to other means of communication.

Orangemen recognise the value of the Holy Bible, the Book of Common Prayer and the Christian literature by which the faith has been proclaimed effectively over the centuries and throughout the world.

Imperial Grand Chaplain 1982-1994,
Honorary Vice President 1994-

Because I have long been convinced of the merit of the written word much of my literary work has been Bible-based, and always there is a Christian perspective in all that I write. That has meant very many devotional essays -'Thought for the Week' for more than forty years in The Mourne Observer newspaper and thirty years plus in The Orange Standard. The selection of these published in book form titled *Think on These Things* (Schomberg Press, 2006) was the first purely religious book of the Orange Institution.

Incidentally articles from the book, and the papers, have appeared regularly in the magazines of the Order in Australia and New Zealand. I have written elsewhere 'Comment' in The Orange Standard and 'Ulster Forum' in The Orange Torch (Scotland).

As I have always sought to describe the Institution honestly, positively, emphasising its influence for good in society, and its potential for making it one of which to be proud – peaceful, prosperous and politically stable – I deplore then the publication of recent books whose authors treat it negatively, unfairly, and in contradiction of claimed impartiality in their treatment of people in the complex environment we share today.

The renewed emphasis, and concentration, on the Christian faith in Orangeism is a welcome return to what was an original intention of Orangemen when the organisation was founded in 1795.

The founders were Churchmen, and clergymen of the Church of Ireland with a few exceptions.

The Ritual of the Loyal Orange Institution was, and is, in its essence indebted to the Book of Common Prayer.

The candidates for membership are made brethren in lodge with a ceremony which requires acceptance of, and subscription to, the Reformed Faith with vows and promises to worship and witness in the practice of that faith. These obligations required, and accepted, are enshrined in the formularies, rules, and regulations of the Institution. They give credence to the claim that ours is a Christian organisation.

Those of us whose first and foremost reason for being Orangemen was to advance the cause of Christ, and promote Christian teaching and thinking on the fundamentals of life and by the Orange Institution, are pleased that our contributions to it in the past and present are seen as presenting the Order at its best in evaluation and motivation.

This writer with a proven presence in a long and continuous campaign to elevate the spiritual, and to diminish the material in the Orange Order thinking and doing, feels impelled to draw attention to the fact that while cognisance is taken of the negative criticism of the organisation even if only by the abrupt dismissal of such attacks, there has been a poor response to, and support of positive presentations of our thinking on matters of concern to us and to people generally.

29

DIOCESAN COUNCIL

My extra parochial commitments have included membership of several church committees among them the Diocesan Council. I was secretary of the Council for Mission for ten years and of the Home Mission Committee of Down and Dromore and Connor for twenty-three years. My annual essay in its reports often produced good debates at both Diocesan Synods. I was secretary of the Lurgan Clerical Union since February 1973. The society has in its membership the clergy of the diocese of Dromore and a few from other dioceses. My many essays read to the LCU have generally been published afterwards.

I was asked to represent the Church of Ireland at conferences among them the World Conference on Christian Education held at Queen's University in July 1962 when eighty-three countries were represented; at Corrymeela Centre 10 to 11 November 1971 when English academics, Drs. Weimer, Bayley and Nicholson discussed *conflict* with the clergy -

Tony Mulvey, Ambrose McAuley (Roman Catholic); Harold Allen, Robert Dickinson (Presbyterian), Brian Hannon, Ernest Long (Church of Ireland); and John Stewart (Methodist).

The Home Mission and Board of Social Responsibility asked Noel Mackey and I to represent our church in an inter-church study with the RUC at police headquarters. The meetings were held on 5 May, 9 June, 10 November 1975, 19 January 1976 and the policemen were Kenneth Newman and John Hermon, successively Chief Constables, and Trevor Forbes, then in Community Relations and later an ACC. Regrettably the Churches failed to produce a report on these meetings the like of which had not taken place previously.

I was a member of the Board of Management of the Association for Promoting Christian Knowledge for a decade and of Diocesan Library Committee for much longer.

The Right Hon. David Bleakley and I were asked to represent the Church of Ireland at an Irish School of Ecumenics Seminar on conflict in Ireland in the Jesuit College at Milltown, Dublin on 22-23 April 1977, when the other churches were represented. We also considered North and South relations, sectarianism and its effect on religion and politics. Taking part were Michael Hurley, founder of the Irish School of Ecumenics, Professors Enda McDonagh (Maynooth) and Kevin Boyle (Galway), Maurice Hayes (then Northern Ireland Community Relations) and David Jenkins, later to be consecrated Bishop of Durham and a well known controversialist.

Three clergymen Michael Mayes (South), Kerry Waterstone (Midlands) and Ernest Long (North) represented the Church of Ireland at the

Nationwide Initiative on Evangelism held at Nottingham University 22 to 26 September 1980. The Irish Presbyterian Church was not represented and the Methodist Church had one delegate Peter Good. While NIE was geared to meet the English situation we were to learn much from the workings of a conference which had its speakers from the Anglican, Roman Catholic, Reformed and Methodist Churches with several groups and agencies represented. There were seminars, workshops and plenary sessions in a campus which happily accommodated a large assembly. I prepared a report on NIE and presented it to the Irish Council of Churches, the Missions Board of the Presbyterian Church, the Council for Mission (Church of Ireland), the Down and Dromore Diocesan Home Mission Committee, and the Lurgan Clerical Union. The report was distributed by the ICC to the several Church committees concerned with evangelism and was published in The Church of Ireland Gazette (30 January 1981).

There had been a consultation on evangelism for the representatives of the main Protestant Churches at Ballyholme Hotel, Bangor, 21 to 22 September 1979 with participation in NIE a consideration. The lack of enthusiasm for what was seen to be an English happening made our meeting an accommodation to those who felt that Ireland should not ignore something which promised to be a step forward in the Church's plans for the conversion of England. A Down and Dromore delegate to the Partners-in-Mission Consultation held a meeting at the Theological College, Dublin, 12-16 September 1977. I reported on it for The Church Times. This first invitation to other branches of the Anglican Communion, and the Lutheran Church in Germany, to look critically at the Church of Ireland with us was a well intended exercise. In the event its effect was small and its findings barely considered.

The second Partners-in-Mission Conference was held at Killeshandra on 23 to 27 November 1983 with the chairman the Bishop of Derry, Jim Mehaffey. My article 'Philosophy of Partners in Mission' was distributed to parishes. The preparatory meeting ensured that some of the mistakes of Partners in Mission One would not be repeated. We were to find other pit falls in this exercise in sharing ideas and experiences. The consultation was hard work for me for one of my chores was to collate the views of groups who had been set to study questions and to provide answers to them. The time allowed me was short and the promised assistance had gone elsewhere. When I passed on my work Jim Mehaffey and Alan Johnston, Press Officer, helped to produce findings which were generally acceptable to the Consultation. They were circulated later with the statement by the External Partners.

A Northern sub-committee set up to study Authority in the Church of Ireland had W.G. Wilson, J.C. Beckett, E. Turner, R. England and S.E. Long. We had several meetings which reached conclusions with their basis in the Bible, Church History, Anglican tradition and practice, with account taken of the divisions in Christianity in Northern Ireland. When the Northern and Southern sub-committees met at the Theological College, Dublin, to compare findings it was to discover that the differences in attitudes made any agreed statement unobtainable.

Another representative engagement meant attendance at an Assembly's College Seminar on 12 April 1978 when the guest speaker was Father John Coventry SJ and his subject 'The True Church'. The Roman Catholics were Ambrose Macauley, M. Hurley, P. McAvoy; Presbyterians, John Barkley, P. Lowry, G. Gray, J. Haire, J. Thompson, D. Gillies; the Church of Ireland men were H. Butler, Bishop of Connor, E. Turner, K. Cochrane and S.E. Long.

The emphasis on clergy/lay renewal involved us in our diocese in study groups by parishes and deaneries. W.G. Neely, the Diocesan Missioner, arranged clergy studies of ministry in England. There was benefit in seeing how clergy elsewhere related to problems akin to our own. My trips were to Evesham, Coventry and Warwick, February 1972; Bristol, Gloucester and Bath, November 1973; Liverpool and Chester, October 1975. I followed my usual practice of writing and illustrating articles on trips away from Ireland.

30

ROLES AND RESPONSIBILITY

I was Rural Dean of Dromore from January 1970 to August 1985 during which I had the exceptional circumstance of being responsible for Magherahamlet Church for two periods of many months each; vacancy duty in Dromore Cathedral and Magheradroll Church coincidentally. I became a canon of Dromore Cathedral by installation on 30 May 1981 when the preacher was Michael Dewar.

The involvement in community affairs meant fighting causes. One such was when Tom Murphy and I with Sam Magowan went on deputation to see the Minister of Education, W.J. Long, about the closures of Garvaghy and Skeagh schools. The discussions were revealing but the result were closures our appeals notwithstanding. We concluded that if the small schools had to close it would be better to have a large central school in Dromara. We lost that plea too, for the education authorities built a new school at Kinallen, two miles from

Dromara, for Garvaghy, Skeagh and Artana pupils. It would appear that the decision of the ministry was justified for the Kinallen school has performed well educationally to prove itself an asset of considerable value to the whole community,

When farmer Hugh Gibson was kept alive after a very severe heart attack by a heart machine, he and his friends persuaded us to help organise a collection to provide the Dromara practice with those machines. I chaired a meeting on 11 September when the appeal was launched and by October £3,871 had been collected from the community. The fund bought the necessary equipment, and being kept open the practice has benefited ever since from the continuing generosity of the people.

We tried from December 1975 to have a children's play area at Church Hill housing estate to save the small children making the dangerous journey across the narrow, Lagan Bridge to the busy village square but despite approaches to council and MPs years later nothing was done.

We encouraged Social Services to open a weekly Senior Citizen's Day Centre in St John's Hall. It began on 10 September 1970 and had the support of the churches. It was a useful and much enjoyed social morning for men and women from an eight miles radius and supplied a recognisable need for friendship among people who were often in danger of being overlooked by society. It also awakened latent activities in arts and crafts. The centre was still active until 1985 and my retirement, but shortly thereafter it was transferred to Hillsborough, a move I would have resisted strenuously. Dromara had always been the least advantaged of the small towns in that area of the country.

Appointed a Justice of the Peace on 30 January 1968 I was constantly made aware of matters of concern in the community. I have no bad memories of my relations with police and people in the area I served.

I preached my farewell sermons in the Dromara and Garvaghy Churches at the Harvest Festivals, October 1985. At social evenings later we were the recipients of valuable and much appreciated gifts. It was nice to leave an incumbency of eight months short of thirty years with the feeling that our friends would have liked us to stay with them.

We moved to a Church of Ireland Housing Association bungalow at Cairnshill Court, Saintfield Road, near to the city but out of it and close enough to fields to feel we were not out of the country.

When I retired on 31 October 1985 I was fortunate to be in my usual good health and anxious to remain busy with my several interests free from the restrictions of full time ministry. To be able to choose, and to refuse, the calls on one's time and services was a new experience. And I was pleased to be invited to continue my ministry part time in Knockbreda Church with occasional Sunday duty elsewhere. I had very happy relations with Desmond McCreery, then rector, who was kind and considerate to us in our breaking into a new way of life. That happy relationship, rector and assisting minister, continued with Philip Patterson who succeeded Desmond in 1989. It has been a privilege to be part of the goodly fellowship of Knockbreda Church.

I always wanted to test my thinking and writing against university standards. I was able to do that when my bishop, Gordon McMullan, advised me about Geneva Theological College, USA and UK, and distance learning. I took a Master of Theology degree in the college with my thesis *The Origin and Influence of the Orange Institution in Ireland since its Inception 1795-1921.* The degree was awarded on 24 November 1988 with the Convocation in King's College, London, on 23 September 1989. I earned a Doctor of Theology degree from Greenwich School of Theology (United Kingdom) with the Convocation at Church House Conference Centre, Westminster, London on 21 September 1991. The thesis was *The Influence of the Orange Institution and the Interactions of Other Movements in Northern Ireland, 1921-1989.*

My third thesis was *An Anglican Perspective on Ecumerism, Evangelism, Politics and Social Justice within the context of Irish Church History and linked to Profiles of Irish Church Leaders – Jeremy Taylor, George Walker, Jonathan Swift, Thomas Percy, Richard Mant, William Alexander and William Shaw Kerr.* For this work I was awarded a Doctor of Ministry degree in 1994.

It was a very large assignment and it meant for me typing every word of manuscripts, each of them of some forty/fifty thousand words. It also meant that I was deeply indebted to Mrs Vera Potter, secretary of Knockbreda Church, and her daughter, Miss Sandra Potter, for photocopying them and to the church for supplying the paper we needed. Without that much appreciated generosity the cost to me would have been considerable.

We enjoyed our special purpose visits to the Dromara and Garvaghy churches. At Garvaghy I dedicated the gifts of the Cunningham family in memory of their parents; and in St John's church on those of the Dromara families, Bailey and Jess, in memory of their parents. After the ceremony presentations were made in St John's Hall to three long serving officers self sacrificing servants of the church, John Jess, Millar Kenny and F.M. Cunningham. It was a privilege to be given the opportunity to pay my compliments to men whom I knew well and for whom I had the greatest respect. They were my fellow labourers in the Gospel and our very good friends.

To think back on the way I have travelled brings emotion of pleasure and pain. There was so much for which to be thankful and so many whose kindness left me constantly indebted to them. My constant regret is that so many of them have departed this life to make me wonder with the actor Kirk Douglas who said, "When nearly all my old friends and colleagues have gone what am I doing here?"

31

UNTIL DEATH DO US PART

The inestimable loss to me was my beloved Ellie, dearest wife, delightful companion and wise friend for nearly sixty years. A lovely lady in appearance and personality I recall when we first met at a church social in the Percy Street Halls of Albert Street Presbyterian Church, Belfast. As was the practice then girls were one side of the hall boys the other. I saw her as one from the rest and was so impressed I asked my friend Billy Knox, later to become a Presbyterian minister in Canada, did he know her. He did and offered to introduce me. We met and talked and I was to echo the words of an old romantic ballad, "*The first time I saw you I knew at a glance that you were the girl for me.*" She was, and when we married after a courtship which endured the war years, lived happily ever after. And the ever after included all the ups and downs of lives often troubled with the constant struggle to live on the meagre salaries of a Church of Ireland curate and rector.

My first year's salary as a married curate was less than what I paid in Income Tax as an aircraft fitter.

To the questions, "To whom are you most indebted as you look back on your life? And who do you most admire from your past relationships and experiences?" The answer to each is "Ellie". She was the wife and mother of such extraordinary ability to be able to do so many things, and to deal with family and everybody so sensibly and sensitively that I was constantly surprised at her longsufferings in dealing with matters that would have required from me the fortitude lack. But the characteristic most essential to her and me in our marriage was her positive attitude in many problems that we had to face when demands were made on us and our resources were limited, governed financially, for a country rector's stipends in the 1950-1985 were poor by any standards. That we managed to rear and educate our sons and to live well and comfortably was due largely to Ellie's meticulous book keeping and careful recording of expenditure in her wee books. One of them a little diary with its data in that economical use of words for which she was well known. A most legible hand writer she never used words unnecessarily. When I went to London in 1946 I promised her I would write to her every day. I kept the promise so faithfully that Miss Ellie Ferris received the letters until in 1949 they were addressed to Mrs Ellie Long. Her replied, eagerly awaited, were as short as mine were long. I made the excuse then and repeat it now I am a writer but not of correspondence by letter. The skills are dissimiliar.

In my early days at St Clement's of ministry, housing was at a premium and we had to do with an apartment, a flat later, but because of their unsuitability when Norman was with us a sharing of their home with the Browns, Lila was Ellie's sister and husband Jimmy. When we went to Willowfield Parish it provided us with a proper house on the Woodstock Road. We were there until the move to Dromara.

Wherever we were Ellie ensured that with her quiet, friendly, kindly disposition she won the love and respect of all those privileged to know her. Our involvement in parish and community meant that there were no barriers to the enjoyment of friendships "across the board." We were happy to be in places where cross-community relations were beyond reproach.

We, as her boys, were the grateful beneficiaries of the talents of a wonderful cook, baker, needlewoman, gardener, and homemaker as were the many to whom she provided hospitality as our guests for this has always been the task of a clergyman's wife.

These were the days when clergy wives were housewives. The situation has been different for years now with many of the ladies working in occupations or professions. Their earning capacity has meant that a change from then to now with a way of living for husband and wife. They live in very different circumstances regulated by a society which has other aspirations and attitudes from what were common to us. I write about Ellie conscious that words are not adequate to express the depths of my feelings for her. And in my knowledge that fulsome praise, a lofty valuation of her abilities and qualities would not have been enjoyed. She was always self-effacing and modest. I make my apology to her but this I have written as a loving tribute however lacking in my use of words to describe what they can only imply at their best.

The question is sometimes asked of an interviewee, "What are you most proud of?" I can answer that as indeed I do when I pay my respects to Ellie my beloved wife of fifty-eight years. About her I use words economically and sensitively. They are never adequate to express the depths of one's feelings. And I mention her pride in our sons: memories of her and them together in childhood youth are vivid in my mind and heart-warming in my remembrances.

A Proud Father with his Sons

Together we maintained and I retain that very close familial bond. Norman was born 7 July 1950, Colin, 20 May 1956 and Mervyn, 18 July 1958. After school and college at eighteen years of age Norman and Mervyn joined the R.U.C in which they each served as officers for thirty years, then retirement, and the pursuit of other interests. Colin travelled another route and that has meant a number of jobs and wide and varied experiences.

Married men Norman and wife June; Colin and Helen with son Adam, and daughter Beth; and Mervyn and Monica with two daughters Rachel and Catherine and son David. Proud of my sons I am no less proud of my daughters-in-law, and the grand-children, none of them little people anymore. The ladies are caring professionals in different occupations. Itself a reason for gratitude, mine and those whom they serve. They know how much I value them for what they mean to me.

I think of Ellie every moment. The loss does not grow less with time. She still speaks to me in how she lived – the most honest person I have ever known – and what she said so wisely, caringly and memorably. We were a very good partnership. She was very good for me and I believe I was good to her.

My regret is that for such a long time we had to be exceedingly careful with what we had of money and kind, most unfortunately when we had a little more to spend Ellie's health prevented us from enjoying more distant travel and entertainment at home. But on balance we had very much for which to be thankful and not much to make us unhappy with our lot.

Ellie had a very deep love for, and devotion to her siblings. The five sisters were the closest of friends and confidants. They were the unmarried Meg and Ness, Lila and Joyce. Lila with her husband Jimmy Brown, had son Samuel and daughter Maureen. Those two and our three fellows were sharers in childhood experiences and adventures in Dromara when the Belfast folk visited us as they did frequently. Their friendship have continued, though Samuel has been a teacher in Adelaide, Australia, for many years. Maureen, always close to Aunt Ellie remains a good friend to me. When the sisters predeceased her Ellie

The Happy Couple

felt their loss acutely. Meg died in December 1974; Lila, May 1990; Ness and Joyce, December 1999; David McCaughrin Joyce's husband had died in March 1993; Ellie, November 2004. 1999 was a terrible year for us. Jimmy Brown had died in August. My brother George had passed away in December 1998.

The relationships of the families are always very good. My siblings were two sisters and brother George. Lily died as the result of a motor-cycle accident in 1950. Jean is very close to me. She and her husband Billy Duke were with their sons Samuel and Billy visitors with us frequently in Dromara days to share with our three in their fun and games. Brother-in-law Billy died. The Longs, George and Doreen, with their boys George and Ernest, were well acquainted, too, with our country environment. Doreen and their sons are constantly in touch with me.

32

To Sum Up On Eighty Years

Before I retired from the incumbency of Dromara and Garvaghy I was invited to join the staff at Knochbreda Church as an Assisting clergyman for we had chosen to live at Cairnshill Court in the Parish. The rector was Desmond McCreery and my friendship with him and the work in the parish was a pleasurable experience which continued with his successor Philip Patterson. After ten years my engagement ended and we continued, and I remain, a member of the Church.

Many enjoy their retirement. I am one of those who find it the more agreeable when I keep myself occupied with things that matter to me and are noted in this book. Perhaps I should be proud of the fact that over the years I have read forty papers to the Lurgan Clerical Union on many subjects – some of them profiles of personalities in Church and State; and thirty-two to the Loyal Orange Lodge of Research on appropriate studies. Many of them have been published as feature articles and booklets.

Reminiscences, by their very nature are selective. They recount what the writer finds worth recall and they omit much that may have had more interest and value at the time but were so pedestrian and ordinary that they do not now merit a mention.

That goes for decisions, events and the every day experiences of a not uninteresting life. There is the desire too, to avoid wordy, and wearisome, detailed descriptions of them.

There are those who are named for the influence and effect they had on me, but there is the very much larger number who earned my respect and gratitude as we shared our lives in whatever situations and locations we found ourselves.

Ingratitude is a grievance in human relationships. It is an impoverishment of our humanity when we fail to respond appreciatively to a kindness shown to us. To express appreciation encourages the giver to continue the proper practice of helpfulness to others, and the receiver to acknowledge that people need each other to help them live out their lives.

My fellow travellers and travel guides have been "all sorts and conditions" of people. So that my positive responses have been to many who differ from me and one another in attitudes, characteristics, religion, and race. We learned and benefited from sometimes unexpected encounters with those who were and remained strangers. Kindnesses little and large are the gifts of all of us.